Learn ARCore - Fundamentals of Google ARCore

Learn to build augmented reality apps for Android, Unity, and the web with Google ARCore 1.0

Micheal Lanham

BIRMINGHAM - MUMDAI

Learn ARCore - Fundamentals of Google ARCore

Commissioning Editor: Amarabha Banerjee
Acquisition Editor: Reshma Raman
Content Development Editor: Onkar Wani
Technical Editor: Vaibhav Dwivedi
Copy Editor: Shaila Kusanale
Project Coordinator: Devanshi Doshi
Proofreader: Safis Editing
Indexer: Priyanka Dhadke
Graphics: Jason Monteiro
Production Coordinator: Shraddha Falebhai

First published: March 2018

Production reference: 1280318

Published by Packt Publishing Ltd.
Livery Place
35 Livery Street
Birmingham
B3 2PB, UK.

ISBN 978-1-78883-040-9

www.packtpub.com

`mapt.io`

Mapt is an online digital library that gives you full access to over 5,000 books and videos, as well as industry leading tools to help you plan your personal development and advance your career. For more information, please visit our website.

Why subscribe?

- Spend less time learning and more time coding with practical eBooks and Videos from over 4,000 industry professionals

- Improve your learning with Skill Plans built especially for you

- Get a free eBook or video every month

- Mapt is fully searchable

- Copy and paste, print, and bookmark content

PacktPub.com

Did you know that Packt offers eBook versions of every book published, with PDF and ePub files available? You can upgrade to the eBook version at `www.PacktPub.com` and as a print book customer, you are entitled to a discount on the eBook copy. Get in touch with us at `service@packtpub.com` for more details.

At `www.PacktPub.com`, you can also read a collection of free technical articles, sign up for a range of free newsletters, and receive exclusive discounts and offers on Packt books and eBooks.

Contributors

About the author

Micheal Lanham is a proven software and tech innovator with 20 years of experience. He has developed a broad range of software applications, including games, graphics, web, desktop, engineering, artificial intelligence, GIS, and Machine Learning applications for a variety of industries. He was introduced to Unity in 2006 and has been an avid developer, consultant, manager, and author of multiple Unity games, graphics projects, and books since. Micheal lives in Calgary, Canada, with his family.

I would like to thank Reshma Raman, my Acquisition Editor, and the rest of the team at Packt Publishing for showing the utmost professionalism and dedication to producing quality books. I would also like to thank the work by the reviewers for all their hard work. At home, I would graciously like to thank my partner, Rhonda, my internal editor/artist, and Ava, my QA tester and part-time model. Finally, I would like to thank my mother for teaching me to be creative with anything. Thanks Mom...

About the reviewer

Neil Alexander is a recent graduate from the University of North Carolina at Charlotte, where he earned a master's in computer science with a specialization in intelligent and interactive systems. As part of his education, he worked on developing several virtual reality demos and data visualization applications. He graduated from the Don Bosco Institute of Technology and has also worked as a research analyst at an IT publishing firm in Mumbai.

He currently works as a data scientist with several Blockchain and cryptocurrency startups in the Washington D.C. area.

> *I'd like to thank my friends and family, with a quick shout out to Govindan K, who was extremely helpful throughout the review process.*

Packt is searching for authors like you

If you're interested in becoming an author for Packt, please visit `authors.packtpub.com` and apply today. We have worked with thousands of developers and tech professionals, just like you, to help them share their insight with the global tech community. You can make a general application, apply for a specific hot topic that we are recruiting an author for, or submit your own idea.

Table of Contents

Preface

Augmented reality applications have moved from novelty to reality, and with the release of ARKit and now ARCore, have become more accessible to the average developer. Now virtually anyone with a grasp of a programming language can quickly build an AR experience using a variety of platforms. Google, with the release of ARCore, has now made this even easier and also provides support for multiple development platforms. This book will guide you through building AR applications using JavaScript and web in mobile with Java/Android and also in mobile with C# / Unity. Along the way, you will learn the fundamentals of building a quality AR experience for your user.

Who this book is for

This book is for any developer who wants to dive into building an augmented reality app with ARCore, but has no background in game or graphic programming. Although the book only assumes the reader has basic high-school level math, the reader should still have a firm grasp of at least one of the following programming languages: JavaScript, Java, or C#.

What this book covers

Chapter 1, *Getting Started*, covers the fundamental concepts any modern AR app needs to tackle in order to provide a great experience to the user. We will learn the basic concepts of motion tracking, environmental understanding, and light estimation.

Chapter 2, *ARCore on Android*, is an introduction to Android development with Android Studio, where we show you how to install Android Studio and set up your first ARCore app.

Chapter 3, *ARCore on Unity*, discusses how to install and build an ARCore app with Unity. This chapter also shows you how to remotely debug an app using the Android development tools.

Chapter 4, *ARCore on the Web*, jumps into web development with JavaScript and focuses on how to set up your own simple web server with Node.js. Then, this chapter looks through the various sample ARCore templates and discusses how to extend those for further development.

Chapter 5, *Real-World Motion Tracking*, extends our learnings from the preceding chapter and extend one of the web examples to add a real-world motion tracking. Not only will this showcase several fundamentals of working with 3D concepts, but it will also demonstrate how ARCore tracks a user's motion.

Chapter 6, *Understanding the Environment*, jumps back to the Android platform and deal with how ARCore understands the user's environment. We will grasp how ARCore identifies planes or surfaces in the environment and meshes them for user interaction and visualization. Here, we will take a look at how to modify a shader in order to measure and colorize the points from the user.

Chapter 7, *Light Estimation*, explains the role that lighting and shadows play in selling the AR experience to the user. We learn how ARCore provides for the estimation of light and how it is used to light the virtual models placed by the user into the AR world.

Chapter 8, *Recognizing the Environment*, is where we cover the basics of Machine Learning and how essential is the technology to the success of the AR revolution. We then look to building a simple neural network that learns through supervised training using a technique called back propagation. After learning the basics of NN and deep learning, we look to a more complex example that demonstrates various forms of Machine Learning.

Chapter 9, *Blending Light for Architectural Design*, covers the building of an AR design app that allows the user to place virtual furniture in the living space or wherever they need to. We also cover how to place and move an object in AR using touch and how to identify when an object is selected. Then, we will extend our lighting and shadows from Chapter 7, *Light Estimation* and provide real-time shadows on the virtual objects.

Chapter 10, *Mixing in Mixed Reality*, is where we introduce mixed reality through the use of inexpensive MR headsets. ARCore is ideally suited for use in these inexpensive headsets since it already tracks the user and monitors their environment internally. We will oversee how to turn our app from a traditional mapping app using the 3D WRLD API for Unity to an AR mapping app, where we will also provide an option to switch to MR and an MR headset.

Chapter 11, *Performance Tips and Troubleshooting*, covers techniques for measuring an app's performance on all the development platforms we deal with. We then talk about the importance of performance and the impact it can have to the various systems. After that, we cover general debugging and troubleshooting tips, where we finish off with a table that covers the most common errors a user may encounter in this book.

To get the most out of this book

These are the things to be remembered in order to use this book to the fullest:

- The reader will need to be proficient in one of the following programming languages: JavaScript, Java, or C#
- A memory of high-school mathematics
- An Android device that supports ARCore; the following is the link to check the list: `https://developers.google.com/ar/discover/`
- A desktop machine that will run Android Studio and Unity; a dedicated 3D graphics card is not explicitly required

Download the example code files

You can download the example code files for this book from your account at `www.packtpub.com`. If you purchased this book elsewhere, you can visit `www.packtpub.com/support` and register to have the files emailed directly to you.

You can download the code files by following these steps:

1. Log in or register at `www.packtpub.com`.
2. Select the **SUPPORT** tab.
3. Click on **Code Downloads & Errata**.
4. Enter the name of the book in the **Search** box and follow the onscreen instructions.

Once the file is downloaded, please make sure that you unzip or extract the folder using the latest version of:

- WinRAR/7-Zip for Windows
- Zipeg/iZip/UnRarX for Mac
- 7-Zip/PeaZip for Linux

The code bundle for the book is also hosted on GitHub at `https://github.com/PacktPublishing/Learn-ARCore-Fundamentals-of-Google-ARCore`. In case there's an update to the code, it will be updated on the existing GitHub repository.

We also have other code bundles from our rich catalog of books and videos available at `https://github.com/PacktPublishing/`. Check them out!

Download the color images

We also provide a PDF file that has color images of the screenshots/diagrams used in this book. You can download it here: https://www.packtpub.com/sites/default/files/downloads/LearnARCoreFundamentalsofGoogleARCore_ColorImages.pdf.

Conventions used

There are a number of text conventions used throughout this book.

CodeInText: Indicates code words in text, database table names, folder names, filenames, file extensions, pathnames, dummy URLs, user input, and Twitter handles. Here is an example: "Scroll down to the draw method and add the following code beneath the identified line."

A block of code is set as follows:

```
void main() {
    float t = length(a_Position)/u_FurthestPoint;
    v_Color = vec4(t, 1.0-t,t,1.0);
    gl_Position = u_ModelViewProjection * vec4(a_Position.xyz, 1.0);
    gl_PointSize = u_PointSize;
}
```

When we wish to draw your attention to a particular part of a code block, the relevant lines or items are set in bold:

```
uniform mat4 u_ModelViewProjection;
uniform vec4 u_Color;
uniform float u_PointSize;
uniform float u_FurthestPoint;
```

Any command-line input or output is written as follows:

```
cd c:\Android
npm install http-server -g
```

Bold: Indicates a new term, an important word, or words that you see onscreen. For example, words in menus or dialog boxes appear in the text like this. Here is an example: "Select **System info** from the **Administration** panel."

 Warnings or important notes appear like this.

Tips and tricks appear like this.

Get in touch

Feedback from our readers is always welcome.

General feedback: Email `feedback@packtpub.com` and mention the book title in the subject of your message. If you have questions about any aspect of this book, please email us at `questions@packtpub.com`.

Errata: Although we have taken every care to ensure the accuracy of our content, mistakes do happen. If you have found a mistake in this book, we would be grateful if you would report this to us. Please visit `www.packtpub.com/submit-errata`, selecting your book, clicking on the Errata Submission Form link, and entering the details.

Piracy: If you come across any illegal copies of our works in any form on the Internet, we would be grateful if you would provide us with the location address or website name. Please contact us at `copyright@packtpub.com` with a link to the material.

If you are interested in becoming an author: If there is a topic that you have expertise in and you are interested in either writing or contributing to a book, please visit `authors.packtpub.com`.

Reviews

Please leave a review. Once you have read and used this book, why not leave a review on the site that you purchased it from? Potential readers can then see and use your unbiased opinion to make purchase decisions, we at Packt can understand what you think about our products, and our authors can see your feedback on their book. Thank you!

For more information about Packt, please visit `packtpub.com`.

Getting Started 1

Welcome to the world of immersive computing and augmented reality with Google ARCore. In this book, we will start with the basics. First, we will cover the basics of **augmented reality** (**AR**) on some important core concepts. From there, we will cover the installation and basics of the three development platforms (Android, web, and Unity) that we will use throughout the book. Next, we will take a more in-depth look at the technical challenges faced by AR developers, including various solutions techniques and for solving them. In the final chapters of the book, we will expand on those skills by developing three example AR and **mixed reality** (**MR**) apps, where we will build a Machine Learning object recognizer, an AR Designer app, and an app that transitions from AR to MR.

 We decided to omit the Unreal platform from this book, not because it is an inferior platform, but quite the opposite. Unreal is a proven and cutting-edge game engine that is well suited for experienced graphic and game developers. However, Unreal and Unity are essentially on par for development features. Therefore, it made more sense to focus on Unity, which is far better suited for learning game and graphic development.

In this chapter, we will begin by quickly covering the fundamental concepts of immersive computing and augmented reality. Then, we will look at the core problems ARCore is designed to address (motion tracking, environmental understanding, and light estimation). Here's a quick look at the topics we will cover in this chapter:

- Immersive computing
- ARCore and AR
    - Motion tracking
    - Environmental understanding
    - Light estimation
- The road ahead

 This book was written with a beta version of ARCore. If you find something different or something that needs to be changed, contact Packt with your errata.

Immersive computing

Immersive computing is a new term used to describe applications that provide an immersive experience for the user. This may come in the form of an augmented or virtual reality experience. While our attention in this book will be primarily focused on building an augmented reality experience, we will highlight techniques that can be used for VR as well. In order to better understand the spectrum of immersive computing, let's take a look at this diagram:

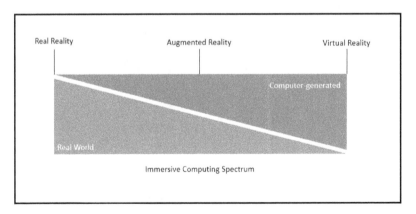

The Immersive Computing Spectrum

The preceding diagram illustrates how the level of immersion affects the user experience, with the left-hand side of the diagram representing more traditional applications with little or no immersion, and the right representing fully immersive virtual reality applications. For us, we will stay in the middle sweet spot and work on developing augmented reality applications. In the next section, we will be introduced to AR and ARCore in more detail.

AR and ARCore

Augmented reality applications are unique in that they annotate or augment the reality of the user. This is typically done visually by having the AR app overlay a view of the real world with computer graphics. ARCore is designed primarily for providing this type of visual annotation for the user. An example of a demo ARCore application is shown here:

Google ARCore demo application: the dog is real

The screenshot is even more impressive when you realize that it was rendered real time on a mobile device. It isn't the result of painstaking hours of using Photoshop or other media effects libraries. What you see in that image is the entire superposition of a virtual object, the lion, into the user's reality. More impressive still is the quality of immersion. Note the details, such as the lighting and shadows on the lion, the shadows on the ground, and the way the object maintains position in reality even though it isn't really there. Without those visual enhancements, all you would see is a floating lion superimposed on the screen. It is those visual details that provide the immersion. Google developed ARCore as a way to help developers incorporate those visual enhancements in building AR applications.

Google developed ARCore for Android as a way to compete against Apple's ARKit for iOS. The fact that two of the biggest tech giants today are vying for position in AR indicates the push to build new and innovative immersive applications.

ARCore has its origins in Tango, which is/was a more advanced AR toolkit that used special sensors built into the device. In order to make AR more accessible and mainstream, Google developed ARCore as an AR toolkit designed for Android devices not equipped with any special sensors. Where Tango depended on special sensors, ARCore uses software to try and accomplish the same core enhancements. For ARCore, Google has identified three core areas to address with this toolkit, and they are as follows:

- Motion tracking
- Environmental understanding
- Light estimation

In the next three sections, we will go through each of those core areas in more detail and understand how they enhance the user experience.

Motion tracking

Tracking a user's motion and ultimately their position in 2D and 3D space is fundamental to any AR application. ARCore allows us to track position changes by identifying and tracking visual feature points from the device's camera image. An example of how this works is shown in this figure:

Feature point tracking in ARCore

In the figure, we can see how the user's position is tracked in relation to the feature points identified on the real couch. Previously, in order to successfully track motion (position), we needed to pre-register or pre-train our feature points. If you have ever used the Vuforia AR tools, you will be very familiar with having to train images or target markers. Now, ARCore does all this automatically for us, in real time, without any training. However, this tracking technology is very new and has several limitations. In the later part of the book, and specifically in Chapter 5, *Real-World Motion Tracking*, we will add a feature to our AR assistant that allows us to track multiple objects' positions from multiple devices in real time using GPS. Then, in Chapter 10, *Mixing in Mixed Reality*, we will extend our tracking to include augmented maps.

Environmental understanding

The better an AR application understands the user's reality or the environment around them, the more successful the immersion. We already saw how ARCore uses feature identification in order to track a user's motion. Yet, tracking motion is only the first part. What we need is a way to identify physical objects or surfaces in the user's reality. ARCore does this using a technique called **meshing**.

We will cover more details about meshing in later chapters, but, for now, take a look at the following figure from Google that shows this meshing operation in action:

Google image showing meshing in action

What we see happening in the preceding image is an AR application that has identified a real-world surface through meshing. The plane is identified by the white dots. In the background, we can see how the user has already placed various virtual objects on the surface. Environmental understanding and meshing are essential for creating the illusion of blended realities. Where motion tracking uses identified features to track the user's position, environmental understanding uses meshing to track the virtual objects in the user's reality. In Chapter 8, *Recognizing the Environment,* we will look at how to train our own machine learning object identifier, which will allow us to extend our meshing to include automatically recognizable objects or areas of an environment.

Light estimation

Magicians work to be masters of trickery and visual illusion. They understand that perspective and good lighting are everything in a great illusion, and, with developing great AR apps, this is no exception. Take a second and flip back to the scene with the virtual lion. Note the lighting and detail in the shadows on the lion and ground. Did you note that the lion is casting a shadow on the ground, even though it's not really there? That extra level of lighting detail is only made possible by combining the tracking of the user's position with the environmental understanding of the virtual object's position and a way to read light levels. Fortunately, ARCore provides us with a way to read or estimate the light in a scene. We can then use this lighting information in order to light and shadow virtual AR objects. Here's an image of an ARCore demo app showing subdued lighting on an AR object:

Google image of demo ARCore app showing off subdued lighting

The effects of lighting, or lack thereof, will become more obvious as we start developing our startup applications. Later, in Chapter 9, *Blending Light for Architectural Design*, we will go into far more detail about 3D lighting and even build some simple shader effects.

In this chapter, we didn't go into any extensive details; we will get to that later, but you should now have a good grasp of the core elements ARCore was developed to address. In the next section, we will take a closer look at how best to use the material in this book.

The road ahead

We will take a very hands-on approach for the rest of this book. After all, there is no better way to learn than by doing. While the book is meant to be read in its entirety, not all readers have the time or a need to do this. Therefore, provided in the following table is a quick summary of the platforms, tools, techniques, and difficulty level of each chapter left in the book:

Chapter	Focus	Difficulty	Platform	Tools and techniques
Chapter 2, *ARCore on Android*	Basics of Android	Basic	Android (Java)	Installation of tools and environment for Android.
Chapter 3, *ARCore on Unity*	Basics of Unity	Basic	Android/Unity (C#)	Installation, setup, and deployment of the Unity sample.
Chapter 4, *ARCore on the Web*	Building ARCore web apps	Medium	Web (JavaScript)	Installation and setup of tools to support web development and hosting.

Chapter 5, *Real-World Motion Tracking*	3D spatial audio and Firebase	Medium	Web (JavaScript)	Introduce motion tracking with a mobile device with audio, integrate with Google Firebase, and track multiple objects and/or users in AR.
Chapter 6, *Understanding the Environment*	Introduction to EU and meshing	Medium	Android (Java)	Learning the ARCore API for Java as well as creating a new ARCore Android project, meshing an environment, and interacting with objects using OpenGL ES.
Chapter 7, *Light Estimation*	Introduction to light estimation and lighting in Unity	Advanced	Unity (C#, Cg/HLSL)	Understand the importance of lighting and how it can be used to make AR objects appear more realistic.
Chapter 8, *Recognizing the Environment*	Introduction to **Machine Learning (ML)** for AR and how it can be used.	Advanced	Android (Java), Unity (C#)	Look at various ML platforms in order to better understand how it can be used in AR applications.
Chapter 9, *Blending Light for Architectural Design*	3D lighting and shaders	Advanced	Unity (C#)	An advanced introduction to lighting and shaders in Unity, including writing HLSL/ Cg shader code.

Chapter 10, *Mixing in Mixed Reality*	Combine all elements together.	Advanced+	Unity (C#), Android (Java)	We will extend the ARCore platform by introducing mixed reality and allowing the app to transition from AR to MR.
Chapter 11, *Performance and Troubleshooting*	Performance and troubleshooting tips	Basic	All	Provides some helpful tips on performance, with a section dedicated to addressing the possible issues you may have while working on the samples.

Also, Chapter 10, *Mixing in Mixed Reality,* is intended to be used after the reader has reviewed all the previous chapters.

While some readers may prefer to only explore a single ARCore platform by sticking to those specific chapters, you are strongly encouraged to work through all the samples in this book. Given that the ARCore API is so similar across platforms, transferring the techniques you learn for one should translate well to another. Also, don't be intimidated by a different platform or programming language. If you have a good base of knowledge in one C language, learning any other language from the rest of the family takes only minimal effort. Developer, programmer, software engineer, or whatever you want to call yourself, you can always benefit from learning another programming language.

Summary

In this chapter, we took a very quick look at what immersive computing and AR is all about. We learned that augmented reality covers the middle ground of the immersive computing spectrum, that AR is just a careful blend of illusions used to trick the user into believing that their reality has been combined with a virtual one. After all, Google developed ARCore as a way to provide a better set of tools for constructing those illusions and to keep Android competitive in the AR market. After that, we learned the core concepts ARCore was designed to address and looked at each: motion tracking, environmental understanding, and light estimation, in a little more detail. Finally, we finished with a helpful roadmap for users looking to get the most out of this book in the shortest amount of time.

In the next chapter, we begin to dive in and get our hands dirty by getting the sample Android project set up and tweaked for our needs.

ARCore on Android 2

Google developed ARCore to be accessible from multiple development platforms (Android [Java], Web [JavaScript], Unreal [C++], and Unity [C#]), thus giving developers plenty of flexibility and options to build applications on various platforms. While each platform has its strengths and weaknesses, which we will get to later, all the platforms essentially extend from the native Android SDK that was originally built as Tango. This means that regardless of your choice of platform, you will need to install and be somewhat comfortable working with the Android development tools.

In this chapter, we will focus on setting up the Android development tools and building an ARCore application for Android. The following is a summary of the major topics we will cover in this chapter:

- Installing Android Studio
- Installing ARCore
- Build and deploy
- Exploring the code

If you have experience working with the Android tools and already have the SDK installed, you may want to just skim over the first three sections. Otherwise, be sure to follow along with the exercises in this chapter, as these steps will be required to undertake exercises in many other areas of this book.

 At the time of writing, in order to perform any of the exercises in this book, you will need an ARCore-supported device. The list of supported devices can be found at https://developers.google.com/ar/discover/ #supported_devices. There has been some work done by others to add support for earlier devices, so if you have an unsupported device, that may be an option. You can find more details about the ARCore for All project at https://github.com/tomthecarrot/arcore-for-all.

Installing Android Studio

Android Studio is a development environment for coding and deploying Android applications. As such, it contains the core set of tools we will need for building and deploying our applications to an Android device. After all, ARCore needs to be installed to a physical device in order to test. Follow the given instructions to install Android Studio for your development environment:

1. Open a browser on your development computer to `https://developer.android.com/studio`.
2. Click on the green **DOWNLOAD ANDROID STUDIO** button.
3. Agree to the **Terms and Conditions** and follow the instructions to download.
4. After the file has finished downloading, run the installer for your system.
5. Follow the instructions on the installation dialog to proceed. If you are installing on Windows, ensure that you set a memorable installation path that you can easily find later, as shown in the following example:

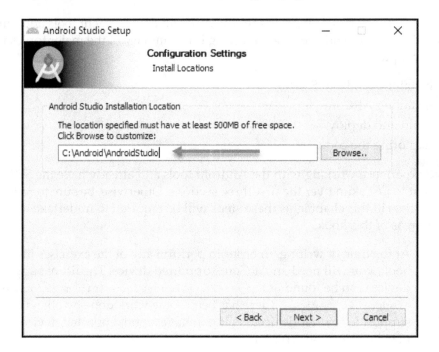

Setting the install path for Windows

6. Click through the remaining dialogs to complete the installation.

7. When the installation is complete, you will have the option to launch the program. Ensure that the option to launch Android Studio is selected and click on **Finish**.

Android Studio comes embedded with OpenJDK. This means we can omit the steps to installing Java, on Windows at least. If you are doing any serious Android development, again on Windows, then you should go through the steps on your own to install the full Java JDK 1.7 and/or 1.8, especially if you plan to work with older versions of Android.

On Windows, we will install everything to `C:\Android`; that way, we can have all the Android tools in one place. If you are using another OS, use a similar well-known path.

Now that we have Android Studio installed, we are not quite done. We still need to install the SDK tools that will be essential for building and deployment. Follow the instructions in the next exercise to complete the installation:

1. If you have not installed the Android SDK before, you will be prompted to install the SDK when Android Studio first launches, as shown:

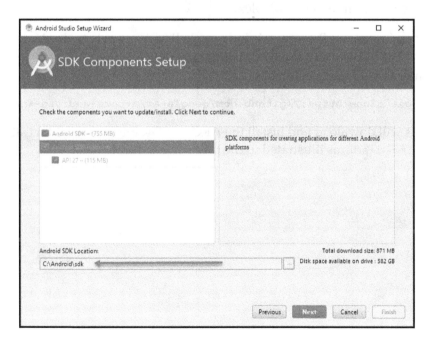

Setting the SDK installation path for Windows

2. Select the SDK components and ensure that you set the installation path to a well-known location, again, as shown in the preceding screenshot.

3. Leave the **Welcome to Android Studio** dialog open for now. We will come back to it in a later exercise.

That completes the installation of Android Studio. In the next section, we will get into installing ARCore.

Installing ARCore

Of course, in order to work with or build any ARCore applications, we will need to install the SDK for our chosen platform. Follow the given instructions to install the ARCore SDK:

 We will use Git to pull down the code we need directly from the source. You can learn more about Git and how to install it on your platform at https://git-scm.com/book/en/v2/Getting-Started-Installing-Git or use Google to search: getting started installing Git. Ensure that when you install on Windows, you select the defaults and let the installer set the PATH environment variables.

1. Open Command Prompt or Windows shell and navigate to the Android (C:\Android on Windows) installation folder.

2. Enter the following command:

```
git clone https://github.com/google-ar/arcore-android-sdk.git
```

3. This will download and install the ARCore SDK into a new folder called arcore-android-sdk, as illustrated in the following screenshot:

```
C:\Android>git clone https://github.com/google-ar/arcore-android-sdk.git
Cloning into 'arcore-android-sdk'...
remote: Counting objects: 73, done.
remote: Total 73 (delta 0), reused 0 (delta 0), pack-reused 73
Unpacking objects: 100% (73/73), done.
Checking connectivity... done.

C:\Android>dir
 Volume in drive C has no label.
 Volume Serial Number is 1834-1598

 Directory of C:\Android

11/04/2017  11:55 AM    <DIR>          .
11/04/2017  11:55 AM    <DIR>          ..
11/03/2017  10:58 PM    <DIR>          AndroidStudio
11/04/2017  11:55 AM    <DIR>          arcore-android-sdk
11/03/2017  11:29 PM    <DIR>          sdk
               0 File(s)              0 bytes
               5 Dir(s)  624,394,555,392 bytes free
```

Command window showing the installation of ARCore

4. Ensure that you leave the command window open. We will be using it again later.

Installing the ARCore service on a device

Now, with the ARCore SDK installed on our development environment, we can proceed with installing the ARCore service on our test device. Use the following steps to install the ARCore service on your device:

NOTE: this step is only required when working with the Preview SDK of ARCore. When Google ARCore 1.0 is released you will not need to perform this step.

1. Grab your mobile device and enable the developer and debugging options by doing the following:
    1. Opening the **Settings** app
    2. Selecting the **System**
    3. Scrolling to the bottom and selecting **About phone**
    4. Scrolling again to the bottom and tapping on **Build number** seven times
    5. Going back to the previous screen and selecting **Developer options** near the bottom
    6. Selecting **USB debugging**

2. Download the ARCore service APK from `https://github.com/google-ar/arcore-android-sdk/releases/download/sdk-preview/arcore-preview.apk` to the Android installation folder (`C:\Android`). Also note that this URL will likely change in the future.

3. Connect your mobile device with a USB cable. If this is your first time connecting, you may have to wait several minutes for drivers to install. You will then be prompted to switch on the device to allow the connection. Select **Allow** to enable the connection.

4. Go back to your Command Prompt or Windows shell and run the following command:

```
adb install -r -d arcore-preview.apk
//ON WINDOWS USE:
sdk\platform-tools\adb install -r -d arcore-preview.apk
```

After the command is run, you will see the word `Success`. If you have encountered an error at this stage, ensure that you consult `Chapter 11`, *Performance Tips and Troubleshooting*, for more help.

This completes the installation of ARCore for the Android platform. In the next section, we will build our first sample ARCore application.

Build and deploy

Now that we have all the tedious installation stuff out of the way, it's time to build and deploy a sample app to your Android device. Let's begin by jumping back to Android Studio and following the given steps:

1. Select the **Open an existing Android Studio project** option from the **Welcome to Android Studio** window. If you accidentally closed Android Studio, just launch it again.

2. Navigate and select the `Android\arcore-android-sdk\samples\java_arcore_hello_ar` folder, as follows:

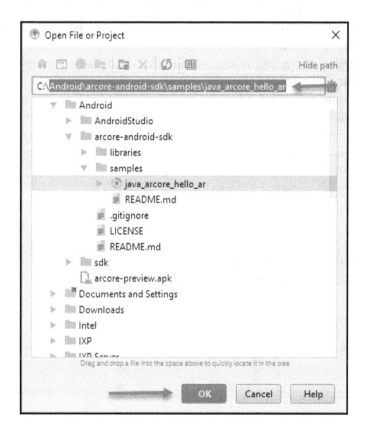

Selecting the ARCore sample project folder

3. Click on **OK**. If this is your first time running this project, you will encounter some dependency errors, such as the one here:

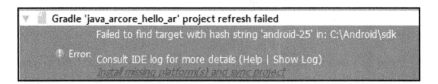

Dependency error message

4. In order to resolve the errors, just click on the link at the bottom of the error message. This will open a dialog, and you will be prompted to accept and then download the required dependencies. Keep clicking on the links until you see no more errors.

5. Ensure that your mobile device is connected and then, from the menu, choose **Run - Run**. This should start the app on your device, but you may still need to resolve some dependency errors. Just remember to click on the links to resolve the errors.

6. This will open a small dialog. Select the **app** option. If you do not see the **app** option, select **Build - Make Project** from the menu. Again, resolve any dependency errors by clicking on the links.

> *"Your patience will be rewarded."*
> *- Alton Brown*

7. Select your device from the next dialog and click on **OK**. This will launch the app on your device. Ensure that you allow the app to access the device's camera. The following is a screenshot showing the app in action:

Sample Android ARCore app running; the dog is real

Great, we have built and deployed our first Android ARCore app together. In the next section, we will take a quick look at the Java source code.

Exploring the code

Now, let's take a closer look at the main pieces of the app by digging into the source code. Follow the given steps to open the app's code in Android Studio:

1. From the **Project** window, find and double-click on the `HelloArActivity`, as shown:

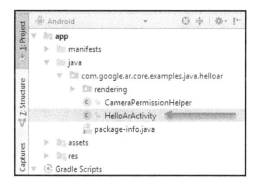

HelloArActivity shown in the Project window

2. After the source is loaded, scroll through the code to the following section:

```
private void showLoadingMessage() {
 runOnUiThread(new Runnable() {
  @Override
  public void run() {
   mLoadingMessageSnackbar = Snackbar.make(
    HelloArActivity.this.findViewById(android.R.id.content),
    "Searching for surfaces...",
    Snackbar.LENGTH_INDEFINITE);
mLoadingMessageSnackbar.getView().setBackgroundColor(0xbf323232);
   mLoadingMessageSnackbar.show();
  }
 });
}
```

3. Note the highlighted text—"Searching for surfaces..". Select this text and change it to "Searching for ARCore surfaces..". The showLoadingMessage function is a helper for displaying the loading message. Internally, this function calls runOnUIThread, which in turn creates a new instance of Runnable and then adds an internal run function. We do this to avoid thread blocking on the UI, a major no-no. Inside the run function is where the messaging is set and the message Snackbar is displayed.

4. From the menu, select **Run - Run 'app'** to start the app on your device. Of course, ensure that your device is connected by USB.

5. Run the app on your device and confirm that the message has changed.

Great, now we have a working app with some of our own code. This certainly isn't a leap, but it's helpful to walk before we run. At this point, go back and review the code, paying special attention to the comments and flow. If you have never developed an Android app, the code may look quite intimidating, and it is. Not to worry, we will deconstruct and reuse several elements of this sample app in Chapter 5, *Real-World Motion Tracking*, and Chapter 6, *Understanding the Environment*.

Summary

In this chapter, we started our exploration of ARCore by building and deploying an AR app for the Android platform. We did this by first installing Android Studio, which will be our go-to **Integrated Development Environment (IDE)** for Android development. Then, we installed the ARCore SDK and ARCore service onto our test mobile device. Next, we loaded up the sample ARCore app and patiently installed the various required build and deploy dependencies. After a successful build, we deployed the app to our device and tested. Finally, we tested making a minor code change and then deployed another version of the app. Doing this assured us that our Android development environment was fully functional, and we are now ready to proceed to the rest of the book.

Our journey continues in the next chapter, where we will build and deploy an ARCore app with the Unity platform. Unity is a leading free/commercial game engine we will use for our final project in `Chapter 10`, *Mixing in Mixed Reality*.

ARCore on Unity 3

The next platform we will set up is Unity. Unity is a leading cross-platform game engine that is exceptionally easy to use for building game and graphic applications quickly. As such, it will be the platform we use when we build our final application in Chapter 10, *Mixing in Mixed Reality*.

 Unity has developed something of a bad reputation in recent years due to its overuse in poor-quality games. It isn't because Unity can't produce high-quality games, it most certainly can. However, the ability to create games quickly often gets abused by developers seeking to release cheap games for profit.

In this chapter, we will learn how to install, build, and deploy Unity ARCore apps for Android. Then, we will set up for remote debugging and, finally, we will explore making some changes to the sample app. The following is a summary of the topics we will cover in this chapter:

- Installing Unity and ARCore
- Building and deploying to Android
- Remote debugging
- Exploring the code

We have already covered setting up the Android tools in Chapter 2, *ARCore on Android*. If you omitted that chapter, you will need to go back and do the exercises in the first few sections before continuing. If you are an experienced Unity developer with an Android environment set up, you should still review this chapter as it may have some useful tips or settings.

Installing Unity and ARCore

Installing the Unity editor is relatively straightforward. However, the version of Unity we will be using may still be in beta. Therefore, it is important that you pay special attention to the following instructions when installing Unity:

1. Navigate a web browser to `https://unity3d.com/unity/beta`.

 At the time of writing, we will use the most recent beta version of Unity since ARCore is also still in beta preview. Be sure to note the version you are downloading and installing. This will help in the event you have issues working with ARCore.

2. Click on the **Download installer** button. This will download `UnityDownloadAssistant`.

3. Launch `UnityDownloadAssistant`.

4. Click on **Next** and then agree to the **Terms of Service**. Click on **Next** again.

5. Select the components, as shown:

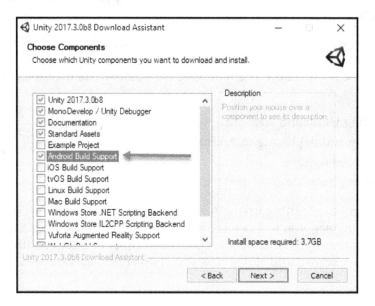

Selecting the components to install

6. Install Unity in a folder that identifies the version, as follows:

Setting the Unity installation path

7. Click on **Next** to download and install Unity. This can take a while, so get up, move around, and grab a beverage.
8. Click on the **Finish** button and ensure that Unity is set to launch automatically. Let Unity launch and leave the window open. We will get back to it shortly.

Once Unity is installed, we want to download the ARCore SDK for Unity. This will be easy now that we have Git installed. Follow the given instructions to install the SDK:

1. Open a shell or Command Prompt.
2. Navigate to your `Android` folder. On Windows, use this:

    ```
    cd C:\Android
    ```

3. Type and execute the following:

    ```
    git clone https://github.com/google-ar/arcore-unity-sdk.git
    ```

4. After the `git` command completes, you will see a new folder called `arcore-unity-sdk`.

 If this is your first time using Unity, you will need to go online to `https:/ /unity3d.com/` and create a Unity user account. The Unity editor will require that you log in on first use and from time to time.

Now that we have Unity and ARCore installed, it's time to open the sample project by implementing the following steps:

1. If you closed the Unity window, launch the Unity editor. The path on Windows will be `C:\Unity 2017.3.0b8\Editor\Unity.exe`. Feel free to create a shortcut with the version number in order to make it easier to launch the specific Unity version later.
2. Switch to the Unity project window and click on the **Open** button.
3. Select the `Android/arcore-unity-sdk` folder. This is the folder we used the `git` command to install the SDK to earlier, as shown in the following dialog:

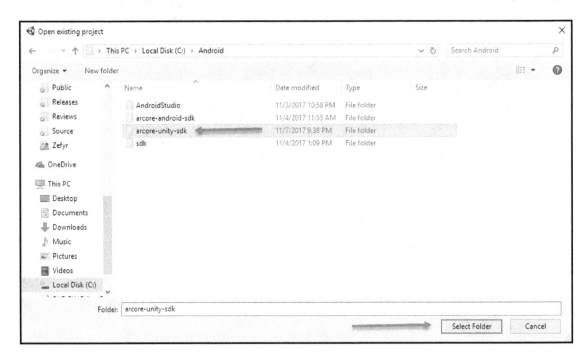

Opening the sample ARCore Unity project

4. Click on the **Select Folder** button. This will launch the editor and load the project.

5. Open the `Assets/GoogleARCore/HelloARExample/Scenes` folder in the **Project** window, as shown in the following excerpt:

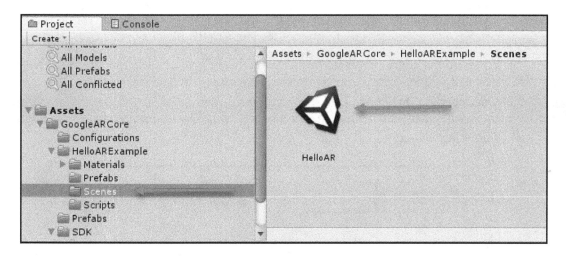

Opening the scenes folder

6. Double-click on the **HelloAR** scene, as shown in the **Project** window and in the preceding screenshot. This will load our AR scene into Unity.

At any point, if you see red console or error messages in the bottom status bar, this likely means you have a version conflict. You will likely need to install a different version of Unity. Consult `Chapter 11`, *Performance Tips and Troubleshooting* for more help.

Now that we have Unity and ARCore installed, we will build the project and deploy the app to an Android device in the next section.

Building and deploying to Android

With most Unity development, we could just run our scene in the editor for testing. Unfortunately, when developing ARCore applications, we need to deploy the app to a device for testing. Fortunately, the project we are opening should already be configured for the most part. So, let's get started by following the steps in the next exercise:

1. Open up the Unity editor to the sample ARCore project and open the **HelloAR** scene. If you left Unity open from the last exercise, just ignore this step.
2. Connect your device via USB.
3. From the menu, select **File | Build Settings.** Confirm that the settings match the following dialog:

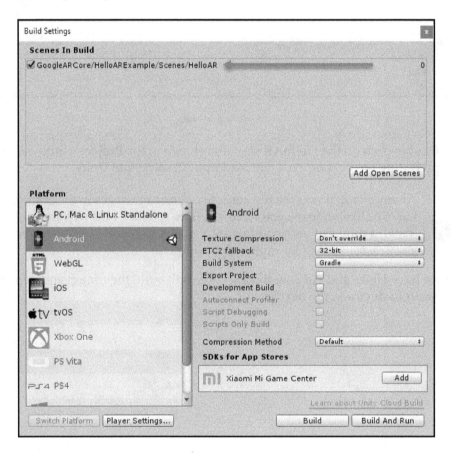

Build settings dialog

4. Confirm that the **HelloAR** scene is added to the build. If the scene is missing, click on the **Add Open Scenes** button to add it.
5. Click on **Build and Run**. Be patient, first-time builds can take a while.
6. After the app gets pushed to the device, feel free to test it, as you did with the Android version.

Great! Now we have a Unity version of the sample ARCore project running. In the next section, we will look at remotely debugging our app.

Remote debugging

Having to connect a USB all the time to push an app is inconvenient. Not to mention that, if we wanted to do any debugging, we would need to maintain a physical USB connection to our development machine at all times. Fortunately, there is a way to connect our Android device via Wi-Fi to our development machine. Use the following steps to establish a Wi-Fi connection:

1. Ensure that a device is connected via USB.
2. Open Command Prompt or shell.

 On Windows, we will add `C:\Android\sdk\platform-tools` to the path just for the prompt we are working on. It is recommended that you add this path to your environment variables. Google it if you are unsure of what this means.

3. Enter the following commands:

```
//WINDOWS ONLY
path C:\Android\sdk\platform-tools

//FOR ALL
adb devices
adb tcpip 5555
```

4. If it worked, you will see `restarting in TCP mode port: 5555`. If you encounter an error, disconnect and reconnect the device.

5. Disconnect your device.

6. Locate the IP address of your device by doing as follows:

   1. Open your phone and go to **Settings** and then **About phone.**
   2. Tap on **Status.** Note down the IP address.

7. Go back to your shell or Command Prompt and enter the following:

   ```
   adb connect [IP Address]
   ```

8. Ensure that you use the IP Address you wrote down from your device.

9. You should see `connected to [IP Address]:5555`. If you encounter a problem, just run through the steps again.

Testing the connection

Now that we have a remote connection to our device, we should test it to ensure that it works. Let's test our connection by doing the following:

1. Open up Unity to the sample AR project.
2. Expand the **Canvas** object in the **Hierarchy** window until you see the **SearchingText** object and select it, just as shown in the following excerpt:

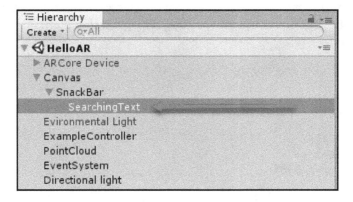

Hierarchy window showing the selected SearchingText object

3. Direct your attention to the **Inspector** window, on the right-hand side by default. Scroll down in the window until you see the text `"Searching for surfaces..."`.

4. Modify the text to read `"Searching for ARCore surfaces..."`, just as we did in the last chapter for Android.

5. From the menu, select **File** | **Build and Run**.

6. Open your device and test your app.

Remotely debugging a running app

Now, building and pushing an app to your device this way will take longer, but it is far more convenient. Next, let's look at how we can debug a running app remotely by performing the following steps:

1. Go back to your shell or Command Prompt.
2. Enter the following command:

   ```
   adb logcat
   ```

3. You will see a stream of logs covering the screen, which is not something very useful.

4. Enter *Ctrl* + *C* (*command* + *C* on Mac) to kill the process.

5. Enter the following command:

   ```
   //ON WINDOWS
   C:\Android\sdk\tools\monitor.bat

   //ON LINUX/MAC
   cd android-sdk/tools/
   monitor
   ```

6. This will open **Android Device Monitor**. You should see your device on the list to the left. Ensure that you select it. You will see the log output start streaming in the **LogCat** window. Drag the **LogCat** window so that it is a tab in the main window, as illustrated:

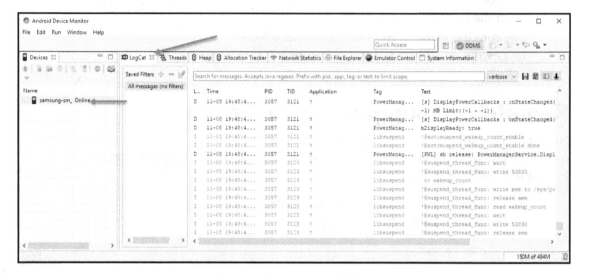

Android Device Monitor showing the LogCat window

7. Leave the **Android Device Monitor** window open and running. We will come back to it later.

Now we can build, deploy, and debug remotely. This will give us plenty of flexibility later when we want to become more mobile. Of course, the remote connection we put in place with `adb` will also work with Android Studio. Yet, we still are not actually tracking any log output. We will output some log messages in the next section.

Exploring the code

Unlike Android, we were able to easily modify our Unity app right in the editor without writing code. In fact, given the right Unity extensions, you can make a working game in Unity without any code. However, for us, we want to get into the nitty-gritty details of ARCore, and that will require writing some code. Jump back to the Unity editor, and let's look at how we can modify some code by implementing the following exercise:

1. From the **Hierarchy** window, select the **ExampleController** object. This will pull up the object in the **Inspector** window.
2. Select the Gear icon beside **Hello AR Controller (Script)** and from the context menu, select **Edit Script**, as in the following excerpt:

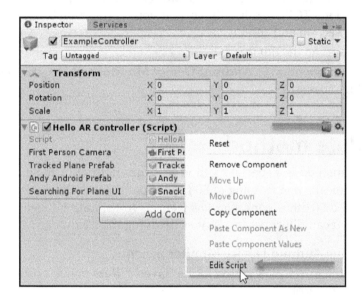

Editing a script in Unity

3. This will open your script editor and load the script, by default, `MonoDevelop`.

Unity supports a number of **Integrated Development Environments** (**IDEs**) for writing C# scripts. Some popular options are Visual Studio 2015-2017 (Windows), VS Code (All), JetBrains Rider (Mac), and even Notepad++(All). Do yourself a favor and try one of the options listed for your OS.

4. Scroll down in the script until you see the following block of code:

```
public void Update ()
{
    _QuitOnConnectionErrors();
```

5. After the `_QuitOnConnectionErrors();` line of code, add the following code:

```
Debug.Log("Unity Update Method");
```

6. Save the file and then go back to Unity. Unity will automatically recompile the file. If you made any errors, you will see red error messages in the status bar or console.

7. From the menu, select **File | Build and Run**. As long as your device is still connected via TCP/IP, this will work. If your connection broke, just go back to the previous section and reset it.

8. Run the app on the device.

9. Direct your attention to **Android Device Monitor** and see whether you can spot those log messages.

Unity Update method

The Unity `Update` method is a special method that runs before/during a frame update or render. For your typical game running at 60 frames per second, this means that the `Update` method will be called 60 times per second as well, so you should be seeing lots of messages tagged as Unity. You can filter these messages by doing the following:

1. Jump to the **Android Device Monitor** window.

2. Click on the green plus button in the **Saved Filters** panel, as shown in the following excerpt:

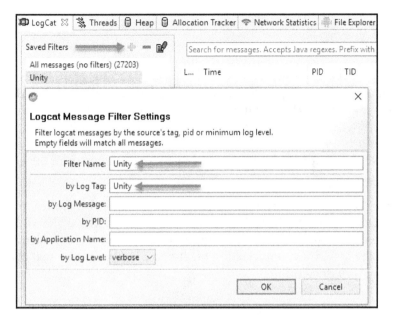

Adding a new tag filter

3. Create a new filter by entering a **Filter Name** (use `Unity`) and **by Log Tag** (use `Unity`), as shown in the preceding screenshot.

4. Click on **OK** to add the filter.

5. Select the new `Unity` filter. You will now see a list of filtered messages specific to Unity platform when the app is running on the device. If you are not seeing any messages, check your connection and try to rebuild. Ensure that you saved your edited code file in `MonoDevelop` as well.

Good job. We now have a working Unity set up with remote build and debug support, which will certainly make our job easier going forward. Now that you have everything set up, go back to Unity platform and get more familiar with the interface. Try not to change any settings as we will use the sample project as our base in later chapters.

Summary

In this chapter, we set up a new platform for our ARCore development, called Unity. Unity, as we learned, is a leading, powerful, flexible, and simple game/graphic engine we will use extensively in later chapters. For now though, we installed Unity and the ARCore SDK for Unity. We then took a slight diversion by setting up a remote build and debug connection to our device using TCP/IP over Wi-Fi. Next, we tested out our ability to modify the C# script in Unity by adding some debug log output. Finally, we tested our code changes using the Android Device Monitor tool to filter and track log messages from the Unity app deployed to the device.

We will continue to grind away in the next chapter and set up our environment for web ARCore development. Web ARCore development is substantially different from Android and Unity. However, we will still cover some essential setup for components we will use in Chapter 10, *Mixing in Mixed Reality*, so don't feel you can bypass the next chapter, even if you are not doing web development.

ARCore on the Web 4

Previously, most AR development would need to be done on a native installed app. Except, with the advent of ARCore, Google has added support for AR development on the web, which, allows users to access AR applications through a browser. Of course, AR web applications may never be as robust or feature rich as a similar app done with Android or Unity. Yet ARCore extends its browser support to include iOS as well as Android. So if you need a cross-platform AR app, then you likely want to focus on ARCore web development.

In this chapter, we continue our work of setting up our environment for ARCore web development. Listed here are the main topics we will cover in this chapter:

- Installing WebARonARCore
- Installing Node.js
- Exploring the samples
- Debugging web apps on Android
- 3D and three.js

Even if you have no interest in web development, you should still review this chapter. We will be using elements from this chapter in the final project, Chapter 10, *Mixing in Mixed Reality*.

Installing WebARonARCore

In order to run ARCore from the web, we also need a browser that supports ARCore or ARKit. At the time of writing (beta preview), no browser supports ARCore or ARKit, and therefore, we need to install a special or experimental browser. The experimental browser we will install is called WebARonARCore.

At the time of writing, Google ARCore is in the beta preview. If Google ARCore is in full release (1.0) and supported in a browser on your device, then you can bypass this section.

Installing WebARonARCore is quite simple and just requires you to point a browser on your device and install an APK. Follow the given steps to install WebARonARCore:

1. Point a browser on your device to `https://github.com/google-ar/` `WebARonARCore` or just Google `git WebARonARCore`.
2. Follow the instructions in the README file to find and click on the **WebARonARCore APK** download link. This will download the APK to your device. If you get a security warning about the APK file type, just bypass it.
3. Click on **Open** after the file downloads. If your device is set to block installation of apps from unknown sources, you will get a warning. To bypass the warning, do this:
    1. Tap on **Settings**.
    2. Tap on **Unknown sources** to enable it.
4. Click on **Install** to install the APK to your device.
5. Locate the **WebARonARCore** app on your device and open it.
6. Tap on **Allow**, through the security warnings.

This will launch the WebARCore experimental browser and point it at the same GitHub page we pulled the APK from. Leave the app open on your device as we will use it in an upcoming section. In the next section, we will learn to install Node.js.

 You can test your web development on an iOS device by installing WebARonARKit. Unfortunately, the code for WebARonARKit source must be built, compiled, and deployed manually. These steps are not covered in this book, but if you are interested in setting up for an iOS device, follow `https://github.com/google-ar/WebARonARKit`.

Installing Node.js

Unlike the other platforms, we don't need to install anything more on the device to use an AR web app. However, we do need a way to serve up our web application pages to a device. Typically, this is done with a web server, like IIS, Tomcat, Jetty, Node, or others. For our purpose, we just need a simple HTTP server to serve up static HTML content. Fortunately, Node provides a package just for running a simple HTTP server from a folder. In order to get this package, we first need to install Node. Follow the given steps to install Node:

1. Download and install the **Long Term Support** (**LTS**) version of Node.js from Nodejs.org. Just follow the instructions on the page and installer. Ensure that you set the PATH when installing to Windows.

 Node.js is a lightweight, non-blocking, and event-driven JavaScript runtime built on top of Chrome's JavaScript runtime. It has become hugely popular due to its massive library of modules or packages. We are installing Node.js just to use a Node.js package.

2. Open Command Prompt or shell and enter the following:

   npm

3. If you have everything installed correctly, you should see a message showing the npm usage.

The Node Package Manager

Node Package Manager (**npm**) is a command-line tool used to install the packages for Node.js. We will use this tool to download and install our simple HTTP server. Follow the given steps to install the HTTP server:

1. From your device, open Command Prompt or shell and enter this:

   npm install http-server -g

2. This will download and install http-server as a global tool. Now, let's test it.

3. Use your Command Prompt or shell and change your folder to `Android`, like this:

```
//WINDOWS
cd c:\Android
```

4. Run `http-server` from the `Android` folder by entering the following:

```
http-server -p 9999
```

5. You will see a list of endpoint URLs. Choose an endpoint that is on the same subnet as your Wi-Fi, the same subnet as your device. Copy or write down the text of the endpoint, as shown in the following excerpt:

```
C:\Android>http-server -p 9999
Starting up http-server, serving ./
Available on:
  http://172.23.210.113:9999
  http://10.0.75.1:9999
  http://10.0.10.200:9999
  http://192.168.1.118:9999  ←
  http://127.0.0.1:9999
Hit CTRL-C to stop the server
[Thu Nov 16 2017 20:41:59 GMT-0700 (Mountain Standard Time)] "GET /" "Mozilla/5.0 (Windows NT 10.0; Win64; x64) AppleWeb
Kit/537.36 (KHTML, like Gecko) Chrome/62.0.3202.94 Safari/537.36"
[Thu Nov 16 2017 20:42:00 GMT-0700 (Mountain Standard Time)] "GET /favicon.ico" "Mozilla/5.0 (Windows NT 10.0; Win64; x6
4) AppleWebKit/537.36 (KHTML, like Gecko) Chrome/62.0.3202.94 Safari/537.36"
[Thu Nov 16 2017 20:42:00 GMT-0700 (Mountain Standard Time)] "GET /favicon.ico" Error (404): "Not found"
[Thu Nov 16 2017 20:42:43 GMT-0700 (Mountain Standard Time)] "GET /" "Mozilla/5.0 (Windows NT 10.0; Win64; x64) AppleWeb
Kit/537.36 (KHTML, like Gecko) Chrome/62.0.3202.94 Safari/537.36"
```

Picking an endpoint URL

6. Open a web browser on your device and enter the endpoint you selected in the preceding step. After you start making connections, you will see the log output shown in the preceding screen excerpt.

If you are unable to connect with your device, ensure that you are entering the full endpoint including the protocol, `http://192.168.1.118:9999` in the example, but your endpoint will likely be different. Ensure that you allow any exceptions in your firewall for port `9999`. Alternatively, you can turn off your firewall for testing. Just don't leave it off.

7. You should see the `Android` folder listing in your browser, as we have configured our server to just list the contents of the `Android` folder. The following is an example of how this will look in your browser:

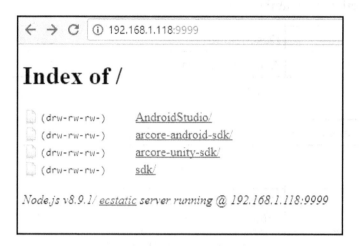

Browser showing the Android folder listing

Good! Now we have a way to simply server up any static web pages we need. In the next section, we will pull down the web ARCore examples and review them.

Exploring the samples

Now that we have an AR-enabled web browser, we can proceed to exploring some examples. Follow the instructions in the mentioned steps to explore the samples:

1. Open Command Prompt or shell to the `Android` folder and enter this:

```
git clone https://github.com/google-ar/three.ar.js.git
```

2. Ensure that your `http-server` web browser is running from the `Android` folder. If you need to start the server again, just run the command from the last exercise.
3. Point your web AR-enabled browser (WebARCore) on your device to a valid endpoint URL. Again, check the last exercise if you forgot how to do this. If the page goes black or is unresponsive, you may have to reset the app. Just shut down the WebARCore browser app and restart it.

4. Browse to the `three.ar.js/examples/` folder. Inside this folder, you will find a set of example HTML pages of AR apps developed with `three.js` and `three.ar.js`. The following table outlines each of the examples, with a description of what they do:

Page	Description	Concepts
`boilerplate.html`	A simple project for building on	Basic
`graffiti.html`	Touch interaction and drawing in AR	Touch, environment
`record-at-camera.html`	Record 3D spatial audio at a point	Touch, spatial audio
`reticle.html`	Tracks the pose of a surface	Motion, pose tracking – environment
`spawn-at-camera.html`	Touch spawn an object at the camera position	Touch, environment
`spawn-at-surface.html`	Touch spawn object on a identified surface or plane	Touch, environment
`surfaces.html`	Identifies surfaces or planes in the environment	Environment

At the time of writing these were the examples available. There likely will be some new samples added that have some of the newer features or other ways of doing things. Be sure to check your folder and spend some time exploring each of those samples.

5. Browse through each of the samples on your device. These samples are excellent examples of the concepts we will cover in the later chapters.

If the screen goes black while running the WebAR browser, then just force close the app and restart it. What typically happens is that Chrome's **Developer tools** (**DevTools**) and the app get out of sync and just need to be restarted.

We now have an HTTP server running on our development machine serving up web AR apps to our device. This is great, but how will we edit the code and debug? Being able to debug code will also be critical to our success when we start writing new code. Therefore, in the next section, we will learn how to set up remote web debugging to an Android device.

Debugging web apps on Android

As we mentioned at the end of the last section, debugging/logging will be critical for us when we start writing new code. If you have ever tried to fix an issue blind without a log or ability to debug, then you will quickly appreciate the value of a good debugger. As it so happens, Chrome has a great set of tools that will help us do just that. Work through the following steps to set up remote web debugging on your Android device:

1. Connect your device to your computer with a USB.
2. Open Command Prompt window.
3. Validate your connection by entering this:

   `adb devices`

4. The output of that command should show your connected device. You may be able to get away with bypassing this step, but you can avoid plenty of frustration later by just running this simple check.
5. Ensure that all instances of the Chrome browser on your Android device are shut down.
6. Open an instance of the WebARCore browser. Remember that this browser is just an experimental extension of Chrome.
7. Using the open browser, navigate to one of the samples. It really doesn't matter which just yet. This example will use `spawn-at-camera.html`.

Connecting Chrome Developer tools

So, believe it or not, we are connected and ready to debug at this point. Now, we just need to set up our debugging tools on the development machine:

1. Open Chrome on your development machine. If you don't have Chrome installed, you will need to do this. Of course, if you are reading a book on Google ARCore, you likely already have Chrome installed, right?
2. Open the Chrome Developer tools by pressing *command + option + I* (Mac), *Ctrl + Shift + I* (Windows, Linux), or from the menu: **More tools** | **Developer tools**.

3. From Chrome's **Developer tools** menu, select **More tools | Remote devices**, as shown:

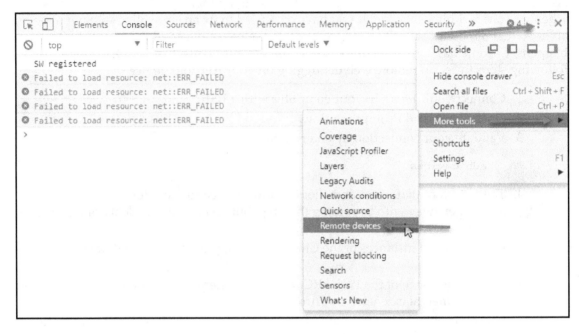

Locating the remote debugging menu option

4. A new tab, **Remote devices**, will open and should show your connected device, as follows:

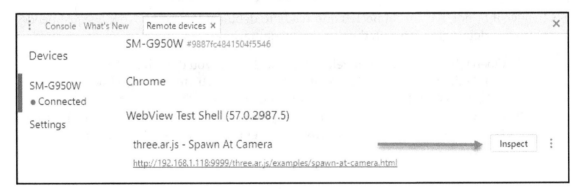

The Remote devices tab showing the connected device and page

5. At the bottom of the tab, you should see the address you are currently pointing to on your device. If this is not the case, there may be a text box allowing you to manually enter it and then connect.

6. Click on the **Inspect** button. This will open a new Chrome window with **Developers Tools** on one side and an image of your device on the other.

Debugging with Chrome

At this point, if you have experience using the Chrome DevTools, you are good to start debugging. Of course, if this is all relatively new to you, follow the given steps to learn how to debug in DevTools:

1. Switch your view to the Chrome window we opened in the last section.
2. Click on the **Sources** tab of the DevTools window.
3. Select `spawn-at-camera.html` or the one you used in your testing.
4. Scroll down through the HTML and JavaScript until you see the `onClick()` function.
5. Click on the line number **229** (**229** in the example, but yours may differ), just left of the highlighted code to set a break point. This is also demonstrated in the following excerpt:

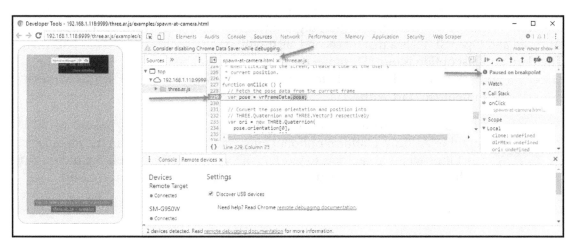

Setting a JavaScript break point

6. Switch back to the device that is running the app. Touch on the screen to spawn an object. When you do this, your app should display a **Paused in debugger** message at the top and then graciously freeze.

7. Switch back to your development machine and the **Developer Tools** window. You will see the app paused at your break point. Now, you can use your mouse to hover over code to inspect variables and anything else you may be debugging.

 Feel free to explore setting other break points and even stepping through the code. We will leave it up to the reader to explore more of the DevTools functionality on their own.

Now you can remote debug an AR web app running on your device. This also completes most of our initial basic setup. We can now get into the details of working with AR in 3D, starting in the next section.

3D and three.js

We live in a 3D world. Therefore, for us to convincingly fool our users into believing that their reality is being augmented or altered, we need to work with their world in three dimensions. Now, each of the platforms we are working with (web, Android, and Unity), all have 3D engines we will be using. In the case of Unity, it is the 3D engine and without a doubt the easiest to use with little or no programming or math knowledge required. Android and OpenGL ES is a distant second, as it will require some knowledge of 3D math. The third and last option is our 3D engine for web, which will be `three.js` library. The `three.js` will be the most difficult platform to work with when using 3D, which makes it our perfect candidate to start with.

 The Unreal platform, as we mentioned in `Chapter 1`, *Getting Started*, is another ARCore platform option. Unreal is similar to Unity in the manner that it provides great tools to work in 3D, although those tools are more technical and will require understanding of 3D maths to be successful.

Unlike in the previous chapters, we will not do just a simple text change to test our ability to change and deploy code. Instead, in this section, we will modify the 3D object we spawn. This will be a good dive into the deep end of 3D and get us ready for the rest of the book. Let's get started by following the given steps:

1. Use a text editor such as Notepad, Notepad++, vi, or something else to open the `spawn-at-camera.html` file located in the `Android/three.ar.js/example` folder.

2. Scroll down in the code until you see the following section:

```
var geometry = new THREE.BoxGeometry( 0.05, 0.05, 0.05 );
var faceIndices = ['a', 'b', 'c'];
for (var i = 0; i < geometry.faces.length; i++)
{
  var f  = geometry.faces[i];
  for (var j = 0; j < 3; j++)
{
    var vertexIndex = f[faceIndices[ j ]];
    f.vertexColors[j] = colors[vertexIndex];
  }
}
var material = new THREE.MeshBasicMaterial({ vertexColors:
                                        THREE.VertexColors });
```

3. Comment out or delete the entire section of code. Use `//` to convert a line as a comment.

4. Enter the new code just before the highlighted line:

```
var geometry = new THREE.TorusGeometry( 10, 3, 16, 100 );
var material = new THREE.MeshBasicMaterial( { color: 0xffff00 } );
cube = new THREE.Mesh(geometry, material);
```

5. This first new line replaces the geometry with a torus. The `TorusGeometry` is a helper function for creating a torus. There are plenty of other helpers for creating many other geometries or even loading mesh objects. The second line creates a new basic single color material. Then, it wraps that material around the geometry and creates our object (mesh), which for now, we will keep calling cube. If you feel the need to change the variable name, then by all means go ahead, but do be careful.

6. Save your code changes.

7. Switch back to your device and refresh the page. Then, tap the screen to spawn the new object. At first, you may think that nothing worked; walk away and move around. You will likely only see the edges of a very large bright yellow torus. If you still have some issues, just ensure that you saved changes and try reconnecting everything.

At this point, we have a number of problems to understand and solve, as outlined in the following list:

- The object is too big or out of scale
- The object is orientated or rotated wrong
- The object needs to be moved or transformed to just in front of the camera
- We want to change the color

Understanding left- or right-handed coordinate systems

While a good understanding of 3D math will certainly be helpful, it isn't entirely essential. All you need to know, for now, is that we define an object in three dimensions (hence, 3D) using a common notation of x, y, and z, where x is the position along the *x* axis, y along *y* axis, and z along *z* axis. Furthermore, we define the position of these axes using a term called left-handed or right-handed coordinate system, as shown in the following diagram:

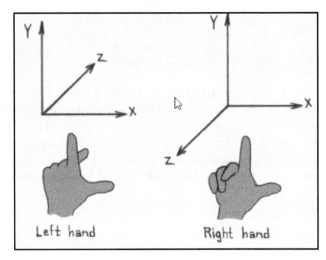

Definition of left-handed and right-handed coordinate systems

Hold up your left hand, as shown in the preceding diagram, and point your middle finger at the screen. Your thumb now points to positive x, your index finger points to positive y, and your middle finger to positive z. Many times, to avoid confusion between left- or right-hand systems, we will just denote the axis by the direction they are pointing. Thus, right is used for positive x, up for positive y, and forward for positive z. Fortunately, for all of our platforms, we will use the left-hand coordinate system.

3D scale, rotation, and transformation

The next thing we need to understand is how to apply scale, rotation, and transformation to an object and thus solve the problems we identified. Without getting deep into the math, let's just understand what those terms mean:

- **Scale**: It allows us to define how large or small an object is. In our example, our object is too big and thus we need to scale the object down. We will learn how to do that shortly.
- **Rotation**: It defines how an object is orientated or posed. We will use both terms interchangeably. Rotation is a bit more complex, and we won't worry about it for this example.
- **Transformation**: It defines the position of an object, where a position of 0,0,0 represents the origin. In our example, we want to position the torus slightly in front of the camera.

We use a mathematical concept called a matrix to apply operations of scale, rotation, and transformation to a 3D object in 3D space. The cool thing about matrices is that they can represent all three operations of scale, rotation, and transformation simultaneously. However, this also means that we have to be careful about the order in which we apply these operations. Let's get back into the code and see how we can apply each of these operations to our torus:

1. Open up your text editor to the `spawn-at-camera.html` example.
2. Scroll to the highlighted code and enter the following lines right after it:

```
scene.add(clone); //near the bottom of the file
clone.scale.copy(new THREE.Vector3(.15,.15,.15));
clone.position.copy(new THREE.Vector3(0,0,10));
```

3. Comment out the line of code beneath that, like this:

```
//clone.position.copy(pos);
```

4. Save your work and run the app in your device. You can now see how we move and scale our spawned object. Feel free to try and move, scale, and even rotate the object further.

As for changing the color from that blinding yellow to something else more appealing, we leave that up to the reader for their homework. Here's the line of code that needs to be changed:

```
var material = new THREE.MeshBasicMaterial( { color: 0xffff00 } );
```

 If you struggled with any of the material in the last section, you really should pick up a book, read a blog/wiki, or take a course on 3D and/or 3D math. Another good option for learning 3D concepts is working with 3D modeling software like Blender, SketchUp, Max, and so on.

We will, of course, cover more 3D concepts throughout the book and in much more detail in the later chapters. For now though, if this is your first exposure to 3D programming, welcome aboard and get ready for a bumpy ride.

Summary

In this chapter, we completed the last of our major setup tasks for the ARCore environments we will explore in later chapters. We first jumped in and installed the prerequisite AR-enabled experimental Chrome browser. Then, we downloaded and installed Node.js as a requirement for running a simple HTTP server. This gave us the ability to pull the examples from the three.ar.js source onto our local machine. We then used the HTTP server to serve up the sample AR web-enabled applications to our device. Next, we tackled the problem of debugging JavaScript code remotely to an Android device. After that, we took a brief tour of 3D and explored ways in which we could scale and transform 3D objects in our AR scenes. Then, we finally learned that good knowledge of 3D concepts and/or math is essential for our success as AR developers.

Now that we are done with the essential setup tasks, it is time to move on to building AR applications of our own. In the next chapter, we will explore the AR concept of motion tracking using our web platform.

Real-World Motion Tracking 5

Now that we have all the fun stuff set up and ready to go, we can begin building some real-world AR apps. In order to do this, we will be picking and choosing various pieces we need from the samples. The samples are great examples, but, for the most part, they are nothing more than boilerplate code. This means that we have no reason to rewrite code sections that already work well. Instead, we will focus on adding new code to tackle AR problems. In this chapter, we will dive in and learn in depth how ARCore motion tracking works. We will learn the current limitations of motion tracking with ARCore and develop a technique for overcoming those limitations. Here are the main topics that we will cover in this chapter:

- Motion tracking in depth
- 3D sound
- Resonance Audio
- A tracking service with Firebase
- Visualize tracked motion

In order to successfully complete the exercises in this chapter, the reader will need to complete the setup till Chapter 4, *ARCore on the Web*. It may be helpful to review some of the exercises from that chapter as well.

Motion tracking in depth

ARCore implements motion tracking using an algorithm known as **visual-inertial odometry** (**VIO**). VIO combines the identification of image features from the device's camera with internal motion sensors to track the device's orientation and position relative to where it started. By tracking orientation and position, we have the ability to understand where a device is in 6 degrees of freedom, or what we will often refer to as the device's/object's **pose**. Let's take a look at what a pose looks like in the following diagram:

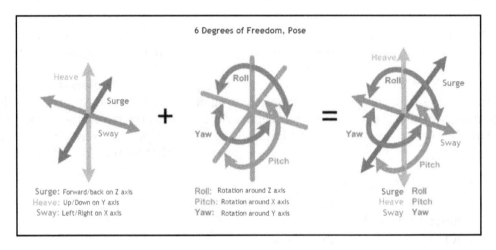

6 Degrees of Freedom, Pose

We will use the term pose frequently when identifying an object's position and orientation in 3D. If you recall from Chapter 4, *ARCore on the Web*, a pose can also be expressed in a mathematical notation called a matrix. We can also refer to rotation in a special form of complex math called a **quaternion**. Quaternions allow us to define all aspects of 3D rotation in a simple form. Again, we won't worry about the specific math here; we will just mention how it is used.

Perhaps it will be more helpful if we can see how this works in a modified ARCore sample. Open up the spawn-at-surface.html example from the Android/three.ar.js/examples folder in a text editor and follow the given steps:

1. Scroll down or search for the update function.
2. Locate the following line of code:

```
camera.updateProjectionMatrix();
```

3. Add the following lines of code right after the highlighted line:

```
var pos = camera.position;
var rot = camera.rotation;
console.log("Device position (X:" + pos.x + ",Y:" + pos.y + ",Z:" +
pos.z + ")");
console.log("Device orientation (pitch:" + rot._x + ",yaw:" +
rot._y + ",roll:" + rot._z + ")");
```

4. Save the file. The code we added just extracts the camera's position and orientation (rotation) into some helper variables: `pos` and `rot`. Then, it outputs the values to the console with the `console.log` function. As it happens, the camera also represents the device's view.

5. Open Command Prompt or shell window.

6. Launch the `http-server` in your `android` folder by entering this:

```
cd /android
http-server -d -p 9999
```

7. Launch the Chrome debugging tools and connect remotely to your device.

8. Open the `spawn-at-surface.html` file using the WebARCore browser app on your device.

9. Switch back to the Chrome tools and click on **Inspect**.

10. Wait for the new window to open and click on **Console**. Move your device around while running the AR app (`spawn-at-surface.html`), and you should see the **Console** tab updated with messages about the device's position and orientation. Here's an example of how this should look:

Console output showing device position and orientation being tracked

The code we added in this example tracks the camera, which, as it so happens, represents the view projected through the device in an AR app. We refer to a camera as the view of a scene in 3D. A 3D scene can have multiple cameras, but, typically, we only use one in AR. The following is a diagram of how we define a camera or view projection in 3D:

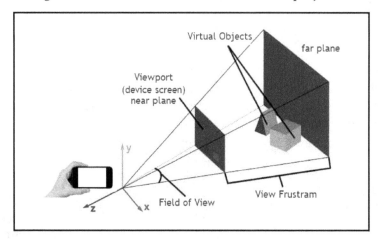

Viewing frustum of a 3D camera

The main task of a camera is to project or flatten the 3D virtual objects into a 2D image, which is then displayed on the device. If you scroll near the middle of the spawn-at-surface.html file, you will see the following code, which creates the camera for the scene:

```
camera = new THREE.ARPerspectiveCamera(
    vrDisplay,
    60,
    window.innerWidth / window.innerHeight,
    vrDisplay.depthNear,
    vrDisplay.depthFar
);
```

Here, vrDisplay is the device's actual camera, 60 represents the field of view, window.innerWidth / window.innerHeight represents the **aspect ratio**, and vrDisplay.depthNear and vrDisplay.depthFar represent the near and far plane depth distances. The near and far, along with the field of view, represent the view frustum. All objects in the view frustum will be rendered. Feel free to try and change those parameters to see what effect they have on the scene view when running the app.

 We use a field of view of 60 degrees in this setting to give a more natural perspective to the objects in the scene. Feel free to experiment with larger and smaller angles to see the visual effect this has on the scene objects.

Now that we have a better understanding of how we can track our device around a scene, we will extend our example. In the next section, we will introduce 3D spatial sound.

3D sound

3D sound is another illusion we cast at the listener in order to further trick them into believing that our virtually generated world is real. In fact, 3D sound has been used extensively for years in movies, TV, and of course, video games in order to trick the listener into a more immersive experience. In a movie, for instance, the listener is stationary, so 3D sound can be mimicked by setting up multiple speakers. However, in an AR or VR mobile app, the sound needs to come from a single (mono) or double (stereo, headphones) source. Fortunately, numerous smart people figured out how our human ears hear using a technique called **binaural sound** to map out sounds in 3D. The next diagram goes into a little more detail on how binaural audio works:

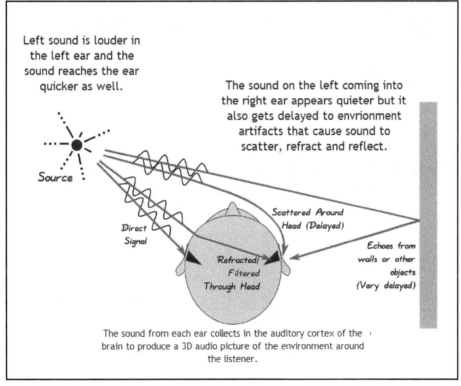

3D sound visualized

Since then, we have figured out not only how to record binaural audio, but also how to play it back, thus giving us the ability to play sounds that fool the brain into thinking that their source is different from reality. However, most of the current technology assumes that the user is stationary, but, of course, that is far from the case in an AR app. In an AR app, our user (listener) is moving in our virtual world, which means that the 3D sounds around the listener also need to adjust. Fortunately, Google has again come to the rescue and developed a 3D sound API for AR and VR, called **Resonance Audio**. We will explore more about Resonance Audio and how to use it in the next section.

Resonance Audio

Google developed Resonance Audio as a tool for developers who need to include 3D spatial audio in their AR and VR applications. We will use this tool to put 3D sound in our demo app. Let's get started by opening up the spawn-at-surface.html file in your favorite text editor and then follow the given steps:

1. Locate the beginning of the JavaScript and add the following lines in the variable declarations:

```
var cube;    //after this line
var audioContext;
var resonanceAudioScene;
var audioElement;
var audioElementSource;
var audio;
```

2. Now, scroll down to just before the update function and start a new function called initAudio, like this:

```
function initAudio(){

}

function update(){   //before this function
```

3. Next, we need to initialize an AudioContext, which represents the device's stereo sound. Inside the initAudio function, enter the following:

```
audioContext = new AudioContext();
```

4. Then, we set up the audio scene in `Resonance` and output the binaural audio to the device's stereo output by adding this:

```
resonanceAudioScene = new ResonanceAudio(audioContext);
resonanceAudioScene.output.connect(audioContext.destination);
```

5. After this, we define some properties for the virtual space around the user by adding the given code:

```
let roomDimensions = {   width: 10, height: 100, depth: 10 };
let roomMaterials = {
    // Room wall materials
    left: 'brick-bare',
    right: 'curtain-heavy',
    front: 'marble',
    back: 'glass-thin',
    // Room floor
    down: 'grass',
    // Room ceiling
    up: 'transparent' };
```

6. As you can see, there is plenty of flexibility here to define any `room` you want. We are describing a room in this example, but that room can also be described as an outdoor space. There's an example of this for the **up** direction at the bottom where the **transparent** option is used. Transparent means sound will pass through the virtual wall in that direction, and you can represent the outdoors by setting all directions to transparent.

7. Now, we add the `room` to the audio scene by writing this:

```
resonanceAudioScene.setRoomProperties(roomDimensions,
                                      roomMaterials);
```

8. Now that `room` is done, let's add the audio source by entering the following:

```
audioElement = document.createElement('audio');
audioElement.src = 'cube-sound.wav';

audioElementSource =
audioContext.createMediaElementSource(audioElement);
audio = resonanceAudioScene.createSource();
audioElementSource.connect(audio.input);
```

9. The `audioElement` is a connection to an HTML `audio` tag. Essentially, what we are doing here is replacing the default audio of HTML with the audio routed through resonance to provide us with spatial sound.

10. Finally, we need to add our `audio` object when we spawn our box and play the sound. Enter the given code just following the function call to `THREE.ARUtils.placeObjectAtHit` inside the `onClick` function:

```
audio.setPosition(cube.position.x, cube.position.y, cube.position.z);

audioElement.play();
```

Before we run our sample, we need to download the `cube-sound.wav` file and put it in our sample folder. Open the folder where you downloaded the book's source code and copy the file from `Chapter_5/Resources/cube-sound.wav` to your `Android/three.ar.js/examples` folder.

 Binaural is so named because we hear sound with both the ears. In order to get the most from the audio examples in this chapter, ensure that you wear stereo headphones. You will be able to hear some differences with your device's mono speaker, but it won't be the same without headphones.

Now when you are ready to run the app, save the `spawn-at-surface.html` page, start your device, and close and reopen the WebARCore app. Play around with the app and spawn a box by tapping a surface. Now when the box spawns, you will hear the cube sound. Move around the scene and see how the sound moves.

Not what you expected? That's right, the sound still moves with the user. So what's wrong? The problem is that our audio scene and 3D object scene are in two different virtual spaces or dimensions. Here's a diagram that hopefully explains this further:

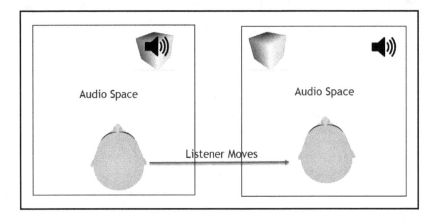

Difference in audio and virtual 3D object space

The problem we have is that our audio space moves with the user. What we want is to align the audio space with the same reference as our camera and then move the listener. Now, this may sound like a lot of work, and it likely would be, if not for ARCore. So thankfully, we can do this by adding one line right after those couple of console lines we put in earlier, like this:

1. Find the two `console.log` lines we added in the previous section and comment them out like this:

> If you omitted the previous section, you will need to go back and complete it. The code we use in this section requires it.

```
//console.log("Device position (X:" + pos.x + ",Y:" + pos.y + ",Z:"
+ pos.z + ")");
//console.log("Device orientation (pitch:" + rot._x + ",yaw:" +
rot._y + ",roll:" + rot._z + ")");
```

2. Add our new line of code:

```
audio.setPosition(pos.x-cube.position.x,pos.y-
cube.position.y,pos.z-cube.position.z);
```

3. All this line does is to adjust the audio position relative to the user (camera). It does this by subtracting the X, Y, and Z values of the position vectors. We could have also just as easily subtracted the vectors.
4. Run the sample again. Spawn some boxes and move around.

Note that when you place a box and move around, the sound changes, as you expect it to. This is due to our ability to track the user in 3D space relative to where a virtual sound is. In the next section, we will look at extending our ability to track users by setting up a tracking service.

A tracking service with Firebase

Now, being able to track a user's motion is all well and good, but what if we wanted to track a user across applications or even multiple users at the same time? This will require us to write a server, set up a database, make a schema, and so on, which is certainly not an easy task and cannot be easily explained in just a chapter. However, what if there was an easier way? Well, there is, and again, Google comes to our rescue with Firebase.

Firebase is an excellent collection of app tools and storage services that are dead simple to use and cross-platform. We will use Firebase database, a real-time database service, to track our user's position. Open up a web browser and follow the given steps:

1. Browse to `firebase.google.com`.
2. Click on the **GET STARTED** button.
3. Log in with your Google (Gmail) account. If you don't have one, yes, you will need to create one to continue.
4. Click on the **Add project** button.
5. Name your project `ARCore` and select your own **Country/Region**, as shown in the following excerpt:

Setting up the ARCore project

6. Click on **CREATE PROJECT**. This will create your project and open up the **Firebase Console**.

7. Click on **Add Firebase to your web app,** which can be found at the top of the **Project Overview** page. This will open up a dialog similar to the following:

```
Add Firebase to your web app                                            ×

Copy and paste the snippet below at the bottom of your HTML, before other script tags.

<script src="https://www.gstatic.com/firebasejs/4.6.2/firebase.js"></script>
<script>
  // Initialize Firebase
  var config = {
    apiKey: "AIzaSyCYEUd7fgSodWI2WqY1AifnbLjPuLnV1xU",
    authDomain: "arcore-4fb70.firebaseapp.com",
    databaseURL: "https://arcore-4fb70.firebaseio.com",
    projectId: "arcore-4fb70",
    storageBucket: "arcore-4fb70.appspot.com",
    messagingSenderId: "1088349741059"
  };
  firebase.initializeApp(config);
</script>                                                    ──────────→   COPY
```

Copy the setup code for your project

8. Click on **COPY**. This should copy the two script tags and contents to your clipboard.

> Don't worry if the keys and URLs you see are different; they should be different.

9. Open up the `spawn-at-surface.html` file in your favorite text editor. Scroll down to just before the last `<script>` tag, the one with the big block of code. Paste the code (*Ctrl* + *V* and *command* + *V* on Mac) you copied earlier.

Setting up the database

With that, we have set up the ARCore Firebase project. Now we want to create our real-time database and set it up for us to connect to. Go back to the **Firebase Console** and follow the given steps to set up a database:

1. Close the configuration dialog that we left open from the last exercise.
2. Click on **Database** on the left-hand side menu.

3. Click on **GET STARTED**. This will create a Firebase Realtime Database with default security turned on. We don't really need authentication at this point, so let's just turn it off.

4. Click on the **RULES** tab. The default security rule is defined with JSON. We want to change this so that our database has public access. Replace the JSON with the following:

```
{  "rules": {     ".read": true,     ".write": true  }}
```

5. Click on **PUBLISH**. You should now see the following security warning:

```
⚠  Your security rules are defined as public, anyone can read or write to your database          LEARN MORE    DISMISS

1 ▾   {
2 ▾     "rules": {
3          ".read": true,
4          ".write": true
5       }
6   }
```

The security warning after turning on public access

6. Click on the **DATA** tab. Leave this tab and the browser window open.

 Turning off security is okay for development prototyping. However, as soon as you go past a prototype, you need to turn security back on. Failure to do this can cost you all manner of heartache, pain, and things you probably can't imagine.

Time to test the connection

Believe it or not, our real-time database service is up and running; now we just want to test our connection by writing a single value to the database from our AR Web app. Open up `spawn-at-surface.html` in a text editor and follow along:

1. Scroll down to the Firebase script we added earlier. Add the following code after the last line:

```
var database = firebase.database();
```

2. The preceding line creates a reference to the database. Now, let's set some data using the following code:

```
firebase.database().ref('pose/' + 1).set({x: 12,y: 1,z: 0});
```

3. Save the file.

Various versions of the `spawn-at-surface.html` page can be found in the book's downloaded source code at `Chapter_5/Examples`.

4. Run the page on your desktop using the **`http://localhost:9999/three.ar.js/examples/spawn-at-surface.html`** URL. At this stage, we are just setting a single point of data when the page starts, as a test, so we don't need AR. Of course, ensure that you start `http-server` before running any tests.

5. After the page loads, you will see the ARCore warning message, but not to worry, this is just a test of the real-time database service.

6. Go back to the **Firebase Console (**`https://console.firebase.google.com/u/0/?pli=1`**)** window we left open. Ensure that you are looking at the **Database** page and **DATA** tab, as shown:

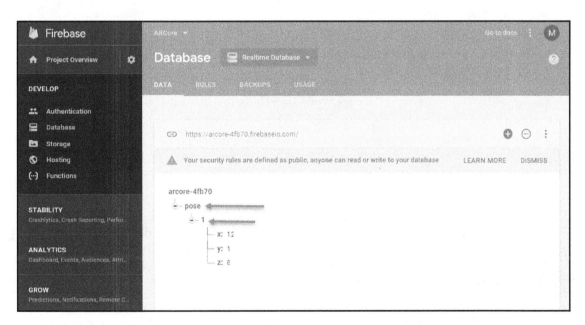

Checking the data that was set on the Firebase database

7. Expand the **pose** and its child objects, as shown in the preceding excerpt. If everything is working correctly, you should see the values we set for a simulated pose (position).

We now have a service in place, with the ability to track any data we want. Firebase allows us to model our data and schema on the fly, which is very useful in prototyping. It also has the extra benefit of being free, public, and accessible from the other platforms we will work with later. In the next section, we will put our tracking service to use by tracking the user in real time.

Visualizing tracked motion

Now that we understand how to track motion and have a service in place, let's see how we can put this service to use and visualize the tracked data in our AR app. Open up the `spawn-at-surface.html` page in a text editor and follow the given steps:

1. Find that last line of code we added in the last exercise and delete it:

```
firebase.database().ref('pose/' + 1).set({x: 12,y: 1,z : 0});
//delete me
```

2. Replace that line with the following code:

```
var idx = 1;
setInterval(function(){
  idx = idx + 1;
  if(camera){
   camera.updateProjectionMatrix();
   var pos = camera.position;
   var rot = camera.rotation;
   firebase.database().ref('pose/' + idx).set({x: pos.x,y: pos.y,z :
pos.z, roll: rot._z, pitch: rot._x, yaw: rot._y });
  }  }, 1000);
```

3. The first line in the preceding snippet is setting an index or count variable. Then, we use the `setInterval` function to set up a repeating timer that calls the anonymous function every second (1000 milliseconds). We do this so that we only track movement every second. We could certainly track movement every frame like in a multiplayer game, but for now, one second will work. The rest of the code, you have seen earlier in the previous exercises.

4. Save the file.

5. Run the sample in your browser's device. Now, move around with the device.

6. Go to the **Firebase Console**. You should now see a stream of data getting fed into the database. Feel free to expand the data points and see the values being captured.

Great, we can now see our data being collected. Of course, it is a little difficult for us humans to easily make sense of the data unless we can visualize it in 2D or 3D, which means that we have a few options. We can build a separate web page to just track the users on a map. Yet, that sounds more like a standard web exercise, so let's leave that to readers who are so inclined. Instead, what we will do is draw a 3D path of where the user has traveled, using the same data that we are sending to our database. Open up that text editor again and load up `spawn-at-camera.html` to follow along:

1. Locate that call to the `setInterval` function we added in the last exercise. We need to change some code in order to create a line from the points.

2. Enter the following code after the identified line:

```
firebase.database().ref('pose/' + ... //after this line
if(lastPos){
  var material = new THREE.LineBasicMaterial({ color: 0x0000ff
});
  var geometry = new THREE.Geometry();
  geometry.vertices.push(
     new THREE.Vector3( pos.x, pos.y, pos.z ),
    new THREE.Vector3( lastPos.x, lastPos.y, lastPos.z )
  );
  var line = new THREE.Line( geometry, material );
  scene.add( line );
}
lastPos = { x: pos.x, y: pos.y, z: pos.z};
```

3. This code first checks whether `lastPos` is defined. On the first run through the `setInterval` timer loop, `lastPos` will be undefined; it then gets set right after the `if` statement. Then, after `lastPos` is defined, we create a basic line `material` with the call to `THREE.LineBasicMaterial`, passing in a hexadecimal color value. Next, we create our `geometry`, a `line`, using the current `pos` and `lastPos` variables with the `material`. We do this by first constructing a `Vector3` object with the x, y, and z values of each position. Finally, we add the `line` to the scene with `scene.add(line)`.

A vector is nothing more than an ordered set of numbers, where each number represents a dimension. There are a number of cool mathematical properties about vectors that are useful to know. However, for now, think of a `Vector3` as representing a point in 3D space at the x, y, and z coordinates. We use the term vertex to refer to a vector or point on a line, surface, or mesh.

4. Save the file and run it in the WebARCore browser on your device. Now when you move around, you will see a trail of blue lines follow you, as shown in the following picture:

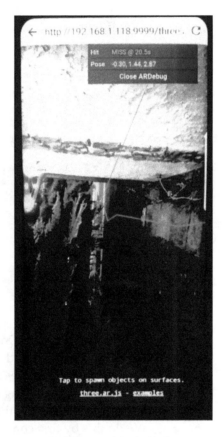

Sample showing tracked path as blue lines

Feel free to continue playing with the app. The development cycle (build, deploy, and run) is quick when developing a simple single page web app, which gives you plenty of opportunities to make quick changes, run them, and then debug easily.

Exercises

At the end or near the end of every chapter, an exercise section will be available to test your knowledge and give you more experience with ARCore. Complete the following exercises on your own:

1. Change the color of the tracking line from blue to red, or another color.
2. Replace the straight line segments with a `SplineCurve`. Hint—you will need to track more than one previous position.
3. Make the cube and/or audio follow the user along the tracked path. Hint—you can use another `setInterval` timer function to move the box every 1.1 seconds (1100 milliseconds) along the path.

Summary

With that, we complete our look at motion tracking with ARCore. As we learned, ARCore gives us the ability to track position and rotation or the pose of a device using feature identification correlated with the device's motion sensors. We then learned why it is important to track the position of a user when building AR apps with 3D sound. This taught us the difference between our audio and virtual (3D) scene and how to convert between references. We then extended our ability to track a user by setting up a Firebase Realtime Database and connected that to our AR app. By doing this, we could now track a single user or multiple users globally. Of course, we didn't have enough time here to build on this further. For now, we finished the app by drawing the user's travel path while the device moves around an area.

In the next chapter, we will jump back to working with Android (Java) and learn more about environmental understanding and various related 3D concepts, which is the next topic on the fundamental AR topics' list.

6
Understanding the Environment

Augmented reality applications are all about enhancing or augmenting the user's reality. In order to do this, we as AR app developers need a set of tools capable of understanding the user's environment. As we saw in the last chapter, ARCore uses **visual-inertial odometry (VIO)** to identify objects and features in the environment, which it can then use to obtain a pose of the device and track motion. However, this technology can also help us identify objects and their pose using the same toolkit. In this chapter, we will explore how we can use the ARCore API to better understand the user's environment. Here's a quick overview of the main topics we will cover in this chapter:

- Tracking the point cloud
- Meshing and the environment
- Interacting with the environment
- Drawing with OpenGL ES
- Shader programming

If you have not downloaded the source code from GitHub, you will need to do so for this chapter. Of course, you will also need to have completed the setup and installation of Android covered in Chapter 2, *ARCore on Android*.

Tracking the point cloud

As we discussed, motion tracking in ARCore is done by identifying and tracking recognizable features around the user. It then uses those points with the device's orientation and accelerometer sensors to keep its tracking updated. Without doing this, the ability to track accurately quickly falls apart. Additionally, we gain the benefit of now tracking multiple points that ARCore identifies as object points. Let's see an example of what these tracking points look like by starting up the sample ARCore Android app again. Follow the given steps to get started:

1. Open **Android Studio**. If you haven't opened any other projects, then it should immediately load the Android ARCore sample project. If not, load the project in the `Android/arcore-android-sdk/samples/java_arcore_hello_ar` folder.

2. Open the `HelloArActivity.java` file and scroll down to the `OnDrawFrame` method, as shown in the following excerpt:

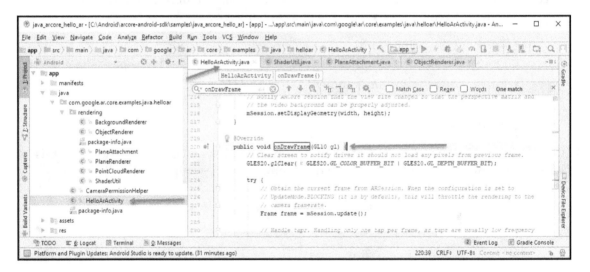

Opening the HelloArActivity.java file in Android Studio

3. OnDrawFrame is the render method, exactly like the update function we have seen in the web example. This method is called every frame, generally around 60 frames per second in the typical 3D app. We also call 60 fps as the frame rate. Frame rates will vary depending on how much your code performs each frame. Therefore, we want our render function and the code inside to be as fast as possible. We will talk more about performance and rendering in Chapter 11, *Performance Tips and Troubleshooting*.

4. The first line in this method, starting with GLES20.glClear, clears the render buffer and prepares for drawing.

 Depending on the 3D platform you are working with, you may or may not have to worry about specific details such as clearing render buffers. Unity, for instance, hides many of these details away from the developer, which can be good and bad. Just understand that all 3D platforms will generally follow the same principals.

5. Scroll down a bit to just inside the try block and add the following line:

```
Frame frame = mSession.update();
```

6. Frame represents the current AR view captured from the device's camera. We get access to an instance of frame by calling mSession.update();mSession, which is initialized earlier, represents our ARCore session service.

7. Frame also exposes a number of helper methods; scroll down until you see the following lines:

```
mPointCloud.update(frame.getPointCloud());
mPointCloud.draw(frame.getPointCloudPose(), viewmtx, projmtx);
```

8. Starting with mPointCloud.update(), this call gets the visible points in the current frame. Then, mPointCloud.draw() draws the points based on the cloud's pose, using the current view (viewmtx) and projection (projmtx) matrices.

 View and projection matrices represent the camera or combined scene view. With three.js, this was handled for us. Likewise, when we get to Unity, we won't need to worry about setting these matrices either.

9. Connect your device to your machine, either through USB or remotely. Then, build and run the app on your device. Pay particular attention to the drawing of the point cloud.

Note how the number of points increases the longer you hold the device in one orientation. These points represent those identifiable and recognizable feature points used for tracking and interpreting the environment. Those are the same points that will help us identify objects or surfaces in the environment. In the next section, we will look at how surfaces are identified and rendered.

Meshing and the environment

So, being able to identify features or corners of objects is really just the start of what we would like to know about the user's environment. What we really want to do is use those feature points to help us identify planes, surfaces, or known objects and their pose. ARCore identifies planes or surfaces automatically for us through a technique called **meshing**. We have already seen how meshing works numerous times in the advanced samples, when ARCore tracks surfaces. Now, before we get ahead of ourselves, let's picture what a point cloud and mesh look like in 3D, with the following diagram:

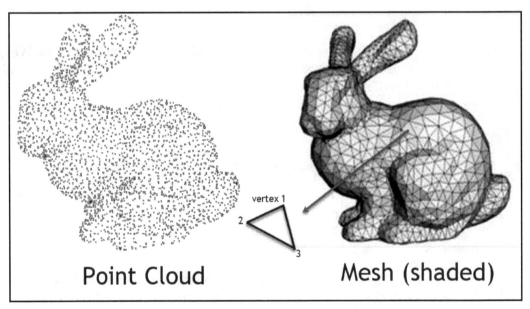

Point cloud and mesh in 3D

If you pay attention to the diagram, you will see an inset figure showing a polygon and the ordered set of vertices that comprise it. Note how the order of points goes counterclockwise. Yes, the order in which we join points makes a difference to the way a surface is facing when a mesh is lit and shaded. When a scene is rendered we only see surfaces that face the camera. Surfaces pointing away from the camera are removed or back-face culled. The order in which we join points is called winding and isn't something you have to worry about unless you plan to create meshes manually.

Meshing is the process of taking a collection of feature points and constructing a mesh from it. The generated mesh is then often shaded and rendered into the scene. If we run the sample right now and watch, we will see the surfaces or plane meshes being generated and placed by ARCore. How about we open up the Android sample project again in Android Studio to see where this meshing occurs:

1. Ensure that your code is open to where we left off last time. You should be looking at the lines with `mPointCloud`.

2. Scroll down just a little until you see this block of code:

```
if (messageSnackbar != null) {
   for (Plane plane : session.getAllTrackables(Plane.class)) {
      if (plane.getType() ==
com.google.ar.core.Plane.Type.HORIZONTAL_UPWARD_FACING
         && plane.getTrackingState() == TrackingState.TRACKING) {
         hideLoadingMessage();
         break;
      }
   }
}
```

3. This block of code just loops through the trackables of type **Plane** (a flat mesh) identified in the session. When it identifies a tracked plane, of the correct type, it hides the loading message and breaks out of the loop.

4. Then, it renders any planes it identifies with this line:

```
planeRenderer.drawPlanes(
    session.getAllTrackables(Plane.class),
camera.getDisplayOrientedPose(), projmtx);
```

5. The `planeRenderer` helper class is for drawing planes. It uses the `drawPlanes` method to render any of the identified planes the ARCore session has identified using the view and projection matrices. You will notice it passes all the planes in through a call to `getAllTrackables(Plane.class)`.

6. Put your cursor on `drawPlanes` and type *Ctrl + B* (*command + B* on Mac) to go to the definition.

7. Now you should see the `drawPlanes` method in the `PlaneRenderer.java` file—don't panic. Yes, there is a lot of scary code here, which, thankfully, is already written for us. As an exercise, just scroll through and read the code. We don't have time to go through it in depth, but reading through this code will give you more insight into the rendering process.

8. From the menu, select **Run - Run 'HelloArActivity'**. Now, as the app runs, pay special attention to the way the surfaces are rendered and how you can interact with them.

Okay, now we understand how surfaces are created and rendered. What we also need to understand is how we interact with those surfaces or other objects in the environment.

Interacting with the environment

We know that ARCore will provide us with identified feature points and planes/surfaces it recognizes around the user. From those identified points or planes, we can attach virtual objects. Since ARCore keeps track of these points and planes for us, as the user moves objects, those that are attached to a plane remain fixed. Except, how do we determine where a user is trying to place an object? In order to do that, we use a technique called **ray casting**. Ray casting takes the point of touch in two dimensions and casts a ray into the scene. This ray is then tested against other objects in the scene for collisions. The following diagram shows how this works:

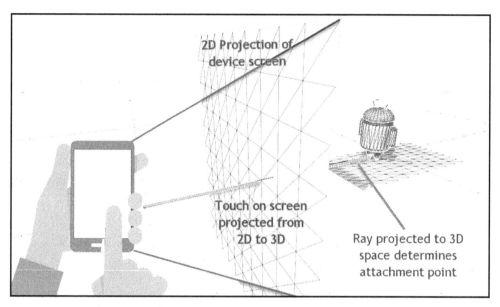

Example of ray casting from device screen to 3D space

You, of course, have likely already seen this work countless times. Not only the sample app, but virtually every 3D application uses ray casting for object interaction and collision detection. Now that we understand how ray casting works, let's see how this looks in code:

1. Open up **Android Studio**, the sample project, and the `HelloArActivity.java` file.

2. Scroll down to the following block of code:

```
MotionEvent tap = queuedSingleTaps.poll();
if (tap != null && camera.getTrackingState() ==
TrackingState.TRACKING) {
  for (HitResult hit : frame.hitTest(tap)) {
    // Check if any plane was hit, and if it was hit inside the
plane
      polygon
    Trackable trackable = hit.getTrackable();
    // Creates an anchor if a plane or an oriented point was hit.
    if ((trackable instanceof Plane && ((Plane)
trackable).isPoseInPolygon(hit.getHitPose()))
        || (trackable instanceof Point
          && ((Point) trackable).getOrientationMode()
            == OrientationMode.ESTIMATED_SURFACE_NORMAL)) {
      // Hits are sorted by depth. Consider only closest hit on a
plane
        or oriented point.
```

```
// Cap the number of objects created. This avoids overloading both the
// rendering system and ARCore.
if (anchors.size() >= 20) {
  anchors.get(0).detach();
  anchors.remove(0);
}
// Adding an Anchor tells ARCore that it should track this position in
// space. This anchor is created on the Plane to place the 3D model
// in the correct position relative both to the world and to the
plane.
anchors.add(hit.createAnchor());
break;
      }
    }
  }
```

3. Read through the comments and pay attention to the highlighted lines of code. The first highlighted line starts a loop based on the number of hits detected in the scene using `frame.hitTest(tap)`. That call is doing the ray casting to determine what objects may be hit by the tap. A **tap** represents the screen touch in 2D.

   The next highlighted line is inside the `if` statement that checks which of the ARCore recognized planes are touched. If there is a hit, we first check that the number of `anchors` is less than 20, where each anchor represents an attachment point. Then we add a new `Anchor` to the collection of `anchors` `ArrayList`, with a reference to a new anchor using `hit.createAnchor`.

4. Scroll down some more to the following block of code in `onDrawFrame`:

```
// Visualize anchors created by touch.
float scaleFactor = 1.0f;
for (Anchor anchor : anchors) {
  if (anchor.getTrackingState() != TrackingState.TRACKING) {
    continue;
  }
  // Get the current pose of an Anchor in world space. The Anchor pose is updated
  // during calls to session.update() as ARCore refines its estimate of the world.
  anchor.getPose().toMatrix(anchorMatrix, 0);

  // Update and draw the model and its shadow.
```

```
virtualObject.updateModelMatrix(anchorMatrix, scaleFactor);
virtualObjectShadow.updateModelMatrix(anchorMatrix, scaleFactor);
virtualObject.draw(viewmtx, projmtx, lightIntensity);
virtualObjectShadow.draw(viewmtx, projmtx, lightIntensity);
```

5. Take a quick read through the code. The first highlighted line starts by looping through the `anchor` in the `anchors` list. We then check whether the anchor is being tracked; if it is, we get its pose in the second highlighted line. Then, we draw our `virtualObject` (**Andy**) in the last lines of code. Note that in this case, we are also drawing shadows.

6. Change the first line of code to match the following:

```
float scaleFactor = 2.0f;
```

7. This change will double the size of **Andy**. Run the app in your device and wait for some surfaces to appear. Then, touch the screen to drop **Andy**. He should now look double the size.

Touch for gesture detection

So, that covers simple interactions. How about we add another gesture to allow the user to clear all the attachment points and thus remove the **Andy** robot from the scene. Follow along the given steps to add another touch gesture:

1. Scroll to the following section of code:

```
// Set up tap listener.
gestureDetector =
    new GestureDetector(
        this,
        new GestureDetector.SimpleOnGestureListener() {
          @Override
          public boolean onSingleTapUp(MotionEvent e) {
            onSingleTap(e);
            return true;
          }

          @Override
          public boolean onDown(MotionEvent e) {
            return true;
          }
        });

surfaceView.setOnTouchListener(
```

```
new View.OnTouchListener() {
  @Override
  public boolean onTouch(View v, MotionEvent event) {
    return gestureDetector.onTouchEvent(event);
  }
});
```

2. The preceding section of code is in the `onCreate` method of the `HelloArActivity`. It first sets up `gestureDetector` for interpreting the selected touch events. Then, we set a listener with `setOnTouchListener` in order to capture touch events and send them to the gesture detector. Just remember that the listener listens for the touch, and the gesture detector interprets the type of touch. So what we want to do is capture another form of gesture from the user.

3. Add the following code right after the highlighted section:

```
@Override
public boolean onDown(MotionEvent e) { return true;} //after this
section

@Override
public void onLongPress(MotionEvent e) {
  onLongPressDown(e);
}
```

4. That sends our event to a new method, `onLongPressDown`. Let's add this new method just below the other gesture handling method by adding the following code:

```
private void onSingleTap(MotionEvent e) {
    // Queue tap if there is space. Tap is lost if queue is full.
    mQueuedSingleTaps.offer(e);
}   //after this block of code
private void onLongPressDown(MotionEvent e) {
    mTouches.clear();
}
```

5. All that happens inside `onLongPressDown` is the collection of `anchors`, `anchors` is cleared. By clearing the `anchors`, we clear the attachment points and thus any rendering of **Andy**.

6. Save the file, connect your device, and run the sample. Try placing a few big **Andy**'s around the scene. Then, use the new long press gesture to remove them.

Good, now we have a basic understanding of how we can interact with the environment. In the next section, we will cover some basics of OpenGL ES, the 3D rendering framework we are using for Android.

Drawing with OpenGL ES

OpenGL ES or just GLES is the trimmed down mobile version of OpenGL. OpenGL is a low-level and powerful 2D and 3D drawing API similar to DirectX. Since it is a low-level library, it does require significant knowledge of 2D/3D maths. Again, for our purposes, we will avoid most of the nasty math and just modify some of the drawing code to change the way the sample app functions. What we will do is modify the sample app to change the way objects are drawn. Load up Android Studio with the sample project and let's get started:

1. Scroll down to the bottom of `PointCloudRenderer.java` and look at the following section of code identified in the following screen excerpt:

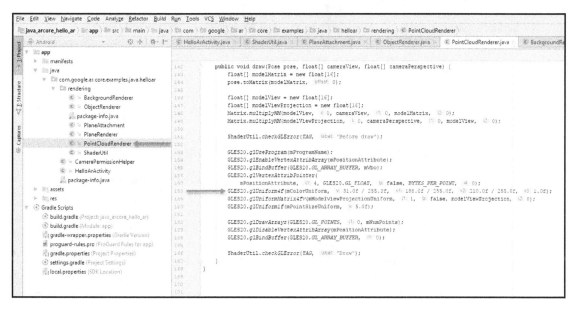

PointCloudRenderer.java open on the draw method

2. Now the code is straightforward, but a lot of what is going on assumes that the developer has a good foundation in 3D maths and graphic rendering. We don't have time to go through every step, but, essentially, all that the code is doing is drawing the identified point cloud features (those blue points).

When we get to the chapters on Unity, you may start wondering why someone would ever put themselves through the pain of writing an AR app with OpenGL ES. That's a good question. Rendering realistic 3D graphics is all about speed and performance. While Unity does an excellent job at rendering, it still is just another layer of software on top of OpenGL ES. This means that Unity would typically run slower than its native OpenGL ES counterpart. How much slower, really depends on what you are trying to do.

3. Take a look at the identified line in the following excerpt, as shown:

```
GLES20.glUniform4f(colorUniform, 31.0f / 255.0f, 188.0f / 255.0f,
210.0f / 255.0f, 1.0f);
```

4. This line sets the color of the rendered point cloud. It does this by normalizing the RGB color values of 31.0, 188.0, and 210.0 by dividing them by 255.0, thus creating a uniform or normalized color vector of values from 0 to 1. With the last value of 1.0 representing the alpha or transparency, where 1.0 means the color is **opaque** and 0.0 means it is **transparent**.

5. Let's experiment a little by changing that line of code to the following:

```
GLES20.glUniform4f(colorUniform, 255.0f / 255.0f, 255.0f / 255.0f,
255.0f / 255.0f, 1.0f);
```

6. Next, we will change the size of points we draw so that they are clearly visible, by changing the following line of code:

```
GLES20.glUniform1f(pointSizeUniform, 25.0f);
```

7. Save the file, connect up your device, and then deploy and run the app. As the app runs, note the color of the points now. Is it what you expected?

Now, we can clearly see how and where the feature points are being identified. However, we still don't get a lot of information from the point data. What if we color the points based on their distance to the viewer? This will allow us to visualize our environment point cloud with some depth information. Doing this in a low-level API such as OpenGL ES to manually subset points by color will require substantial code changes. Fortunately, we can even go lower and write a program called a **shader** to change the color of the point just before we draw it. We will take a dive in to shader programming in the next section.

Shader programming

Shader programming is probably one of the most difficult and low-level development tasks you can do as a graphics programmer. It requires an excellent knowledge of 3D math and the graphics rendering process. Also, writing good shaders is a skill that can take years to master. So why are we covering this in a book that covers fundamentals? Simply put, coding a good shader may be difficult, but it is also extremely rewarding, and it's a skillset that is essential to any serious 3D programmer.

 We will be using shaders throughout the rest of this book for many things. If, at this point, you are starting to feel overwhelmed, then take a break and study some 3D math or jump ahead a chapter. Sometimes, you just need time for things to sink in before you get that eureka moment.

A shader program runs directly on the **graphic processing unit** (**GPU**) of the device or computer. If the device doesn't have a GPU, then the program is executed on the CPU, which is a much slower process. After all, the GPU has been optimized to run shader code and do it extremely well. In fact, virtually all 3D rendering done on the GPU runs the shader code. When we use Unity, a much higher-level game engine, we will still write our own shaders because of the power and flexibility it gives us.

So, what does a shader program look like? The following is an example of a shader written in the **OpenGL Shading Language** (**GLSL**):

```
uniform mat4 u_ModelViewProjection;
uniform vec4 u_Color;
uniform float u_PointSize;

attribute vec4 a_Position;

varying vec4 v_Color;

void main() {
    v_Color = u_Color;
    gl_Position = u_ModelViewProjection * vec4(a_Position.xyz, 1.0);
    gl_PointSize = u_PointSize;
}
```

This is the shader program we use for rendering our point cloud points or vertices. Specifically, this shader is responsible for rendering a single vertex for each call to `main`, and it's called a vertex shader. Later in the rendering process, after the 3D scene is flattened to a 2D image with the vertex shaders, we have the opportunity to run a fragment or pixel shader. A fragment shader is run for every pixel/fragment that needs to be rendered.

Shader programs come in a few variations, but since they all derive from a C language and share so many similar functions, switching from one language to another isn't as difficult as you think. We will, in fact, learn some basics of the GLSL and the form used in Unity called **High Level Shading Language** (**HLSL**), which has its roots in DirectX.

If you look in the `main` function, you will see we are setting three variables: `v_Color`, `gl_Position`, and `gl_PointSize`. Those variables are global and just determine the color, size, and position of the vertex. The first line sets the color to an input variable—`u_Color`. Then, the position is calculated by multiplying the `u_ModelViewProjection` matrix with a new vector representing the position. That operation converts our vertex from world space to screen space. Finally, we set the point size with another input—`u_PointSize`.

What we want to do is modify that shader program so that it colorizes the points based on the distance from the user. Before we do that, though, let's take a look at how the shader gets those inputs. Open up Android Studio to `PointCloudRenderer.java` and follow along:

1. Scroll down to bottom of the `createOnGUIThread` method and look for the following lines:

```
positionAttribute = GLES20.glGetAttribLocation(programName,
"a_Position");
colorUniform = GLES20.glGetUniformLocation(programName, "u_Color");
modelViewProjectionUniform =
GLES20.glGetUniformLocation(programName, "u_ModelViewProjection");
pointSizeUniform = GLES20.glGetUniformLocation(programName,
"u_PointSize");
```

2. Those lines of code set up our shader input positions. What we are doing here is determining the indexes we need for injecting data into the array buffer we pass to the shader. We need to add another input, so add the following line at the end of the preceding code snippet:

```
furthestPoint = GLES20.glGetUniformLocation(programName,
"u_FurthestPoint");
```

3. This line adds another input variable called `u_FurthestPoint`. We need to calculate the furthest point from the user (camera) in order to colorize the points on a gradient. Before we do that, go back to the top of the file and declare the following new variables under the line identified:

```
private int numPoints = 0;    //after this line
private int furthestPoint;
private float furthestPointLength;
```

4. Remember that `furthestPoint` is an index to the variable and `furthestPointLength` will be used to hold the distance to the furthest point.

5. Scroll down to the `update` method and enter the following code after the identified line:

```
numPoints = lastPointCloud.getPoints().remaining() /
FLOATS_PER_POINT;    //after me

furthestPointLength = 1;
if(numPoints > 0) {
    for(int i=0; i<numPoints*FLOATS_PER_POINT;i=
i+FLOATS_PER_POINT) {
        float x = lastPointCloud.getPoints().get(i);
        float y = lastPointCloud.getPoints().get(i+1);
        float z = lastPointCloud.getPoints().get(i+2);
        double len = Math.sqrt(x*x+y*y+z*z);
        furthestPointLength = Math.max(furthestPointLength,
(float)len);
    }
  }
}
```

6. This code first sets our minimum distance (1) to `mFurthestPointLength`. Then, we check whether there are any observed points. If there are, we loop through the points in the point cloud. In the loop, we use the `get` method to index into the point buffer and extract the x, y, and z of the points. This allows us to measure the length of the vector with x, y, and z of the point. You make recognize the equation as the Pythagorean theorem, but in 3 dimensions rather than the 2 you may be used to. We then check whether this new length (distance) is greater than the current furthest length with `Math.max`. Keep in mind that this code is run in the `update` method and thus executed every rendered frame.

We calculate the distance between two points in 3D space using the following formulae:

$$distance = \sqrt{(x_1 - x_2)^2 + (y_1 - y_2)^2 + (z_1 - z_2)^2}$$

Since our camera (user) is the origin, we can assume that one of our points is (0,0,0), which is equal to this:

$$distance = \sqrt{(x_1 - 0)^2 + (y_1 - 0)^2 + (z_1 - 0)^2}$$

This becomes the following:

$$length = \sqrt{x^2 + y^2 + z^2}$$

7. Scroll down to the `draw` method and add the following code beneath the identified line:

```
GLES20.glUniform1f(mPointSizeUniform, 25.0f);   //after me

GLES20.glUniform1f(furthestPoint, furthestPointLength);
```

8. This call sets the `furthestPointLength` that we calculated in the `update` method to the shader program.

Editing the shader

Okay, so that's all the Java code we need to write in order to calculate and set our new distance variable. Next, we want to open up the shader program and modify the code for our needs. Follow the given steps to modify the shader program:

1. Open the `point_cloud_vertex.shader` file under the `res/raw` folder, as shown:

>

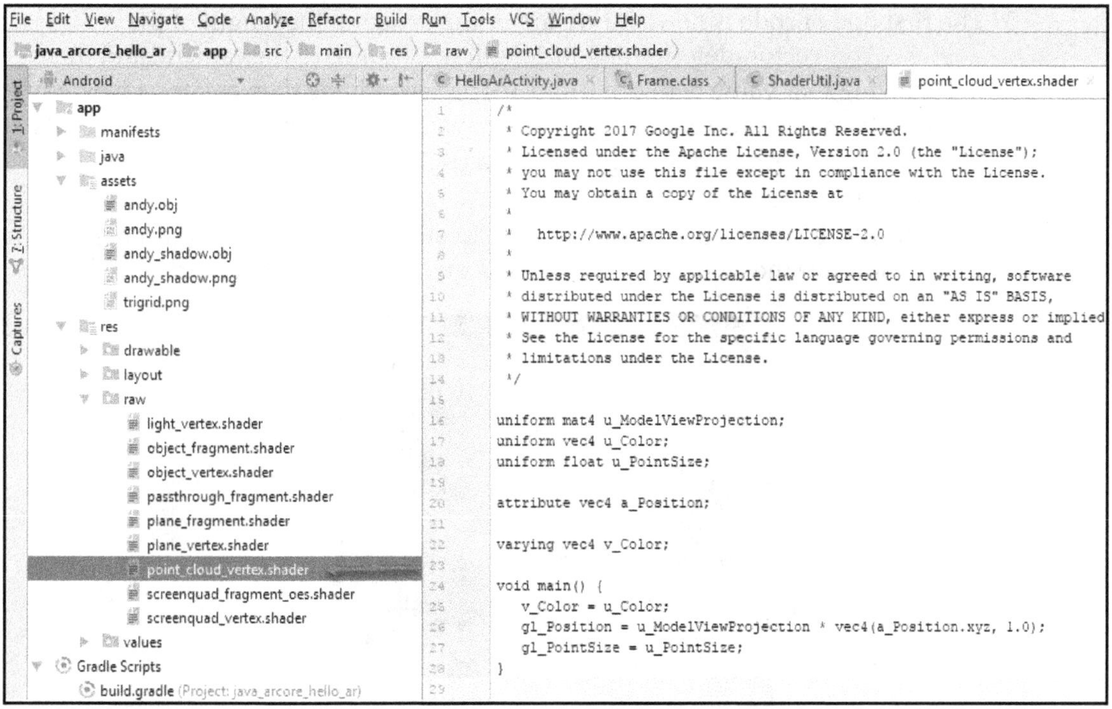

Opening point_cloud_vertex.shader

2. Make the highlighted code changes, as follows:

```
uniform mat4 u_ModelViewProjection;
uniform vec4 u_Color;
uniform float u_PointSize;
uniform float u_FurthestPoint;

attribute vec4 a_Position;

varying vec4 v_Color;

void main() {
    float t = length(a_Position)/u_FurthestPoint;
    v_Color = vec4(t, 1.0-t,t,1.0);
    gl_Position = u_ModelViewProjection * vec4(a_Position.xyz, 1.0);
    gl_PointSize = u_PointSize;
}
```

3. The first line of code is new. All we are doing is taking the length of the `a_Position` vector, determining its length or distance to the camera, and then normalizing that value between 0 and 1. The second line then creates a new `vec4` for color based on our calculations of the `t` variable. This new vector represents the color in the form **red blue green alpha** (**RGBA**), where alpha is set to a constant of `1.0`.

4. Save the file, connect your device, and build and run the app on your device. You should now see the cloud points colorized by distance to the camera, as follows:

Screenshot of colored point cloud points by depth

Imagine if we had to write Java code in order to do the same colorization of the points. We would certainly need a lot more code than what we wrote. Also, any Java code we used would certainly be much slower than a shader. Now, for our example, the app's performance is less critical, but when you develop a real AR app, you will want to squeeze all the performance you can; that's why our discussion and knowledge of shaders is so important.

Exercises

The following exercises are meant to test your skills and the knowledge you just earned in order to build on the work we just completed. Complete the following exercises on your own:

1. Change the color of the tracking line from blue to red, or another color.
2. Replace the straight line segments with a `SplineCurve`. Hint, you will need to track more than one previous position.
3. Make the cube and/or audio follow the user along the tracked path. Hint—you can use another `setInterval` timer function to move the box along the path every 1.1 seconds (1100 ms).

Summary

We began this chapter by first reviewing some concepts on environment tracking and exploring how ARCore keeps track of the environment. Then, we moved on to meshing and how it is used to generate planes and surfaces. From there, we moved on to interacting with the environment, where we saw how a touch gesture is interpreted and converted into a position in a 3D scene. After that, we learned some basics about OpenGL ES and how our point cloud is rendered. We then took a deep dive and introduced the low-level rendering process of shaders. With this, we then modified the point cloud vertex shader in order to colorize the points by distance.

Lighting is a critical element to the whole illusion of augmented reality. In the next chapter, we will dive back into Unity and learn about light estimation.

Light Estimation

7

Magicians spend hours in front of a mirror, watching and studying every angle of their performance in order to get it just right. They realize that every detail needs to be perfect in order for the audience to believe in the illusion. Even a single mistake can ruin not only the illusion, but the entire performance and credibility of the magician. As harsh as it is, this is no different to what it's like building an AR app. If your app will immerse a user in your world, you need to make it as believable as possible. This includes ensuring that all the virtual objects in a scene look like they belong. Magicians use lighting and perspective tricks to fool the user into believing that something is real. We have already seen how we use perspective, so now we need to cover and enhance our use of lighting.

In this chapter, we will cover how ARCore uses light estimation techniques to make the AR experience more believable to the user. We will then go on to extend some of those basic techniques in order to improve our future AR apps. Here are the main topics we will cover in this chapter:

- 3D rendering
- 3D lighting
- Light estimation
- Cg/HLSL shaders
- Estimating light direction

We will use Unity in this chapter because it provides an easier platform for learning about the rendering process, lighting, and more about shader programs. The shader programs in Unity are a different variety and are definitely worth taking a look at.

While this chapter is less than halfway through the book, a reader should consider this as an advanced chapter. We will again be covering more about shader programs and 3D math concepts. Here's a good site for those of you who want to review or just get a basic understanding of 3D math, through this tutorial, *3D Math: Vector Math for 3D Computer Graphics* at `http://chortle.ccsu.edu/vectorlessons/vectorindex.html`. This is an excellent site licensed by *Bradley Kjell*.

3D rendering

Before we get into talking about light estimation for AR, let's step back and review the rendering process of a 3D model. Take a look at the following diagram that explains the rendering process at a high level:

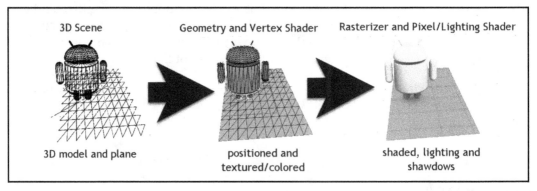

Typical rendering process for a 3D model

Now, the diagram only visually demonstrates the rendering process. Geometry and vertex shaders never actually render a wireframe model. Rather, they only position and color vertices and surfaces, which are then fed into the pixel/fragment and lighting shaders. This last step is called **rasterization** and represents the final step when the 2D image is generated or rasterized.

 The rendering process we are talking about here is for standard real-time rendering on a device's GPU using DirectX or OpenGL. Keep in mind that there are other rendering processes used for real-time (voxel) and non real-time (ray tracing) rendering.

Euclideon have developed a voxel-like rendering technology, which they are claiming to be, in their words, as follows:

"The First Truly Applicable Hologram Tech is Here."

- Euclideon

This sounds very promising and a game changer for AR and VR. However, this technology has come under incredible scrutiny for making, what some feel are outlandish claims of rendering trillions of points without frame rate loss.

Building a test scene

As always, let's take a look at how this looks in our tools. Open up Unity with the sample ARCore project we have already installed, and perform the following steps:

1. From the menu, select **File** | **New Scene**. This will create a new empty scene for us in Unity.
2. From the **Project** window, drag the **Andy** prefab from the Assets/GoogleARCore/HelloARExample/Prefabs folder into the **Hierarchy** window, as shown in the following screen excerpt:

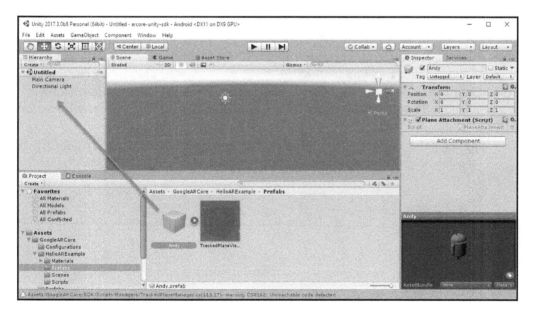

Unity interface showing Andy prefab dragged onto the scene

3. **Andy** is quite small, so we will adjust his size and the camera so that he fits in the **Scene** and **Game** windows better. Select **Andy** and modify **Transform Scale** to **X** as 25, **Y** as 25, and **Z** as 25. Then, select **Main Camera** and modify its **Transform Position** to **Y** as 4. This is shown in the following screen excerpt:

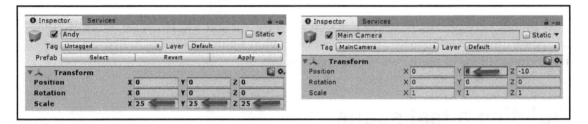

Setting the Transform of Andy and the Main Camera

4. Click on the **Game** and **Scene** tabs to switch views and see how the **Andy** model looks in each view.

The **Scene** window in Unity is for composing your scene objects. This is where you will generally do most of your work in Unity. The **Game** window represents the view, as close as possible, as it is rendered in game. Unfortunately, for ARCore apps, we are limited to testing on a device and thus unable to generate an accurate game view. This is why, for now anyway, we will work in a separate scene for discovery purposes.

5. From the menu, select **GameObject | 3D Object | Plane**. This will add a new plane to the scene. Ensure that the plane is positioned at 0,0,0 by clicking on the Gear icon beside the **Transform** component in the **Inspector** window and selecting **Reset Position** from the menu. After you do that, **Andy** will be casting a shadow on the plane.

6. Switch between views again. Expand the **Shaded** dropdown just under the **Scene** tab, as shown in the following excerpt:

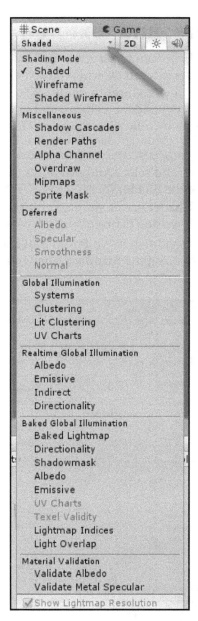

The Draw Mode menu

7. This menu represents the various **Draw Modes** Unity can support. Some of these may make sense, such as **Wireframe**, while others less so. In any case, run through the list of each option to see what they do.

Materials, shaders, and textures

Okay, now we have seen how Unity renders a scene and the various draw modes available. However, we still need to go over how an object is colored or textured. In Unity, we typically use materials, shaders, and textures to render 3D objects. A material is essentially an encapsulation of a shader, its dependent textures, and other settings. Let's see what **AndyMaterial** looks like in Unity by following the given steps:

1. Open the `Assets/GoogleARCore/HelloARExample/Materials/Andy` folder in the **Project** window and select **AndyMaterial**. Look at the **Inspector** window and note the name of the **Shader** (`ARCoreDiffuseWithLightEstimation`) at the top. The current **Shader** uses a simple lighting model and has been optimized for mobile AR, which we don't currently need, so we will change it.

2. Expand the **Shader** dropdown in **AndyMaterial** and select **Standard**. This will switch the material to using the **Standard Shader**, as shown in the following screenshot:

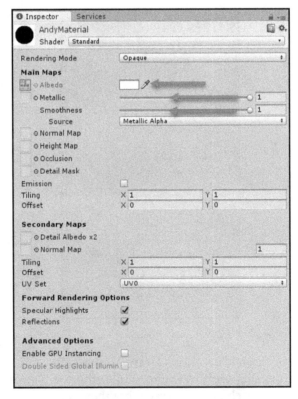

Switching Andy to use the Standard Unity shader

3. The first thing you will immediately note is that **Andy** gets very dark. This is because the **Metallic** and **Smoothness** are turned way up. Use your mouse to adjust the various values to something more pleasant, as shown by the red arrows in the preceding screenshot. Perhaps a metallic shiny **Andy**?

 One thing to note when adjusting materials is that any changes you make to a material will be automatically saved and persisted even when running in the play or demo mode. Sometimes, it is useful to have backups of settings, especially if you found them difficult to achieve.

4. Make a copy of **AndyMaterial** by selecting it in the **Project** window and typing *Ctrl + D* or *command + D* on Mac. Rename the new material **StandardAndyMaterial**.
5. Select **AndyMaterial** again. Change **Shader** back to ARCore/DiffuseWithLightEstimation. Note how the look of **Andy** quickly changes.
6. From the menu, select **File | Save Scenes**. Save the scene to the Assets/GoogleARCore/HelloARExample/Scenes folder as RenderingTest.scene.

As you can see, there are plenty of options and settings that can go into rendering a 3D object. Feel free to explore on your own what each of the material settings are on the **Standard Shader**. In the next section, we will expand our understanding of rendering by discussing lighting.

3D lighting

So far, we have looked at the basics of the rendering process and how a 3D model is rendered. What we omitted in the first section, however, is how lighting plays into this. In order to get a sense of the importance of lights in a 3D scene, how about we go ahead and turn out the lights. Open up Unity to where we left off in the first section and follow along:

1. Select the **Directional Light** object in the **Hierarchy** window.
2. Disable the **Light** in the **Inspector** window by unchecking the box beside the object's name. This will turn off or disable the light. You will note that not all the lights go off, however. This is because we have an ambient or global light that is used to account for general light scattering.

3. You are now left with a dark object with no lights and shadows. Turn back on the **Directional Light** by clicking on the checkbox. Take a look at the properties of the **Light** in the **Inspector** window, as shown:

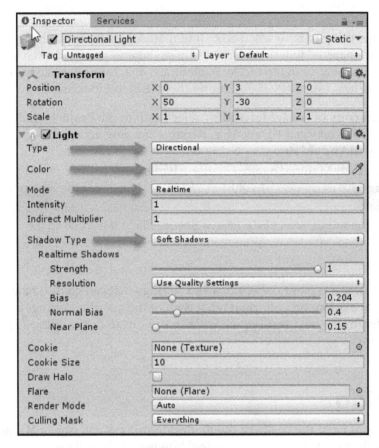

Directional Light properties in the Inspector window

4. Play with the **Type, Color, Mode,** and **Shadow Type** properties in the **Inspector** window. There are four different types of lights you can work with. The **Directional** type represents a light source such as the sun, and as such, we only need to identify the direction the light is pointing. For the other light types, such as **point** and **spot**, you will need to position the light in the scene correctly in order to see any effects.

We can calculate simple 3D diffuse lighting with the following equation:

$$I = -L_D \bullet N$$

Here:

L_D is the direction of the light

N is the normal to the surface

I is the intensity of light [0 to 1]

I is then multiplied by the color in order to determine the resulting lit color.

5. The **Standard Shader** we looked at earlier uses **Physically-Based Rendering (PBR)** or a lighting model, which is quite sophisticated. Unfortunately, PBR shaders are currently limited for mobile platforms and often don't work or have poor performance. Often, the devices' GPU cannot support the additional instructions required for a PBR shader. Therefore, we will be limited to writing our own custom lighting shaders.

6. Let's explore switching shaders on our **AndyMaterial** so that we can see what effect different lighting models have. Locate **AndyMaterial** in the `Assets/GoogleARCore/HelloARExample/Materials/Andy` folder and select it.

7. Switch between `ARCore/DiffuseWithLightEstimation`, **Mobile Diffuse**, and the **Standard** shaders to see the effects or the different lighting models, as illustrated:

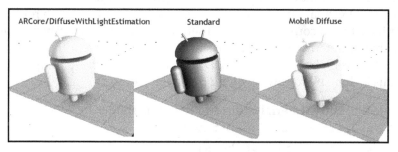

Comparison of lighting models from three different shaders

8. Obviously, the **Standard** shader looks the most natural, but as we learned, PBR shaders are currently not supported on mobile platforms. Another option would be the **Mobile Diffuse** shader; let's see how that shader looks in our AR sample app.

9. Switch the shader to the **Mobile Diffuse** one and then save the project (**File | Save Project**).

10. Connect your device and type *Ctrl + B, command + B* on Mac. This will build and run the app on your device. Play with the app and wait for a surface to be visible and then tap and place **Andy**.

Note anything different about our friend? That's right, he appears to stick out like a hot day in Canada. The reason for this is that the **Mobile Diffuse** shader is assuming a consistent light source, which means our model is always getting the same light (direction and intensity), except that in the real world, as the user moves, light direction and intensity can change dramatically. Your device's camera will try and compensate for this, but you can still see perceptible changes in lighting, especially if the lighting around the user changes dramatically. You can see this by running the app again, and this time, take a closer look at how the lighting looks different on and around our model. ARCore solves this issue of inconsistent lighting by performing a process called light estimation. We will cover light estimation in detail in the next section.

Light estimation

Light estimation is a technique for replicating the lighting conditions of the real world and applying it to our 3D virtual objects. Ideally, we would like to be able to replicate the exact lighting conditions, but of course, we're not there yet. ARCore currently uses an image analysis algorithm to determine light intensity based on the current image from the device. This is then applied as global light to the 3D objects in the scene. Open up Unity again and let's see how this is done by following along the given steps:

1. Locate the **AndyMaterial** again and revert its shader to `ARCore/DiffuseWithLightEstimation`.

2. Save the project (**File | Save Project**).

3. Connect your device and type *Ctrl + B* (*command + B* on Mac) to build and run the app on your device. Place a couple of **Andy** models and alter the lighting conditions. Note how our objects respond to the changes in lighting.

4. Go back to Unity and double-click on the `HelloAR` scene in the `Assets/GoogleARCore/HelloARExample/Scenes` folder to open the scene. Feel free to save your `RenderingTest` scene.

5. Direct your attention to the **Hierarchy** window and double-click on **Directional Light** to focus and highlight it in the **Scene** window. Note how the light is pointing straight down in the **Scene** window. In the **Inspector** window, you will see that the **Shadow Type** is set to **No Shadows**, and the **Intensity** is turned down to 0.7, which essentially turns the light into a directional ambient or global light.

6. Direct your attention back to the **Hierarchy** window and select **Environmental Light**. Go to the **Inspector** window and click on the Gear icon beside the **Environmental Light (Script)** component. Then, select the **Edit Script** option from the context menu, as shown:

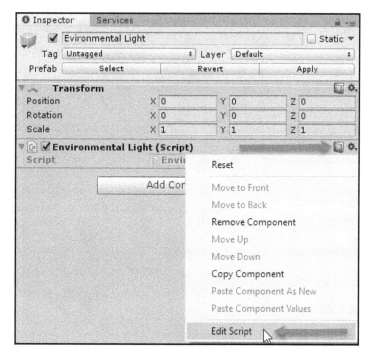

Editing the Environmental Light script

7. This will open up the script in your script editor. By default, Unity installs **MonoDevelop**, which will open the script if you have not installed and set a different editor. Scroll down to the Update method, as follows:

```
public void Update()
{
#if UNITY_EDITOR
        // Set _GlobalLightEstimation to 1 in editor, if the value
is not set, all materials
```

```
            // using light estimation shaders will be black.
            Shader.SetGlobalFloat("_GlobalLightEstimation", 1.0f);
    #else
            if (Frame.TrackingState != FrameTrackingState.Tracking)
            {
                return;
            }

            // Use the following function to compute color scale:
            // * linear growth from (0.0, 0.0) to (1.0,
    LinearRampThreshold)
            // * slow growth from (1.0, LinearRampThreshold)
                const float LinearRampThreshold = 0.8f;
                const float MiddleGray = 0.18f;
                const float Inclination = 0.4f;

            float normalizedIntensity =
    Frame.LightEstimate.PixelIntensity / MiddleGray;
            float colorScale = 1.0f;

            if (normalizedIntensity < 1.0f)
            {
                colorScale = normalizedIntensity * LinearRampThreshold;
            }
            else
            {
                float b = LinearRampThreshold / Inclination - 1.0f;
                float a = (b + 1.0f) / b * LinearRampThreshold;
                colorScale = a * (1.0f - (1.0f / (b *
    normalizedIntensity + 1.0f)));
            }

            Shader.SetGlobalFloat("_GlobalLightEstimation",
    colorScale);
    #endif
        }
    }
```

8. The `#if UNITY_EDITOR` is a compiler directive that checks whether the code is running in the editor. The reason we do this is so that when the code runs in the Unity editor, we want it to ignore any light estimation calculations. When the code is running in the editor, it will execute the next line; the `_GlobalLightEstimation` shader variable is set to 1. This means that when the code is running in the editor, all it does is set our light to 1.0.

You will come across the `#if UNITY_EDITOR` directive quite frequently when doing mobile development. This directive allows you to write test code that only executes when the code is running in the editor. This allows us to simulate the object running in the editor without the need to worry about ARCore services or device restrictions.

9. Direct your attention to the `#else` block of code. This is code that is executed on the device and first checks whether the `Frame` is tracking. We have already seen this check in Android. The rest of the code is essentially just math, but if you look at the last highlighted line, you will see a call to `Frame.LightEstimate.PixelIntensity`. This is the call where ARCore reads the image from the camera and determines the current pixel intensity; a float value from 0 for a totally black image to 1 that is fully white. The intensity is normalized based on a constant called `MiddleGray`. The `MiddleGray` color or light intensity of `0.18f` corresponds roughly to the point where we humans stop recognizing colors.

10. We then use the `normalizedIntensity` to determine whether we want a linear change in lighting, when `normalizedIntensity` is less than `1.0`, or more gradually, when the intensity is greater than `1.0`. That's all that the rest of the math is doing, just making the lighting change more gradually after a certain threshold.

11. Change the `MiddleGray` constant to match the following line:

```
const float MiddleGray = 1.0f;
```

12. This will convert our light estimation to now use a linear model. Save the code change and return to Unity. Unity will automatically recompile the code and inform you of any errors in the status bar at the bottom of the editor.

13. Connect your device and build and run. Place an **Andy** on a surface. Note how dark the figure is; this is because the lighting model is too abrupt.

 We are using a single channel of color or what you may also call gray scale. This is why we refer to values as a color but it is in fact just a single float. A gray scale color of `0.18f` is equivalent to the RGB color (`0.18f`, `0.18f`, `0.18f`) or what ARCore calls `MiddleGray`.

14. Change the `MiddleGray` constant back to `0.18f`, save the project, and run the app. Note the difference in lighting.

This covers how ARCore uses image analysis techniques to read the light intensity from the camera's image and converts that value into a global light intensity or color. The lighting value is set on a shader, and we will follow how that value is used in the next section.

Cg/HLSL shaders

The shading language used in Unity is a variety of HLSL, or sometimes referred to as Cg. This shading variant provides two different forms of shaders: **surface** and **vertex/fragment** shaders. Now, coming from Android, this may sound confusing, since GLSL treats vertex and fragment shaders differently. However, variety of HLSL in Unity treats vertex and fragment shaders as the same, since they reside in the same file and are in the same workflow. A surface shader, which handles the lighting of our model, can be simple or quite complex. The Standard Unity surface shader uses a PBR lighting model, which is quite advanced and not supported on most mobile devices. This issue, combined with our limited ability to track scene lights, limits us to writing our own shaders in order to get our object lighting correct. ARCore provides us with a very simple surface shader that is used in the sample to light the **Andy** model. Let's open up Unity and take a look at what that shader looks like by following the given steps:

1. Load up the `HelloAR` sample project and scene.
2. Select the **AndyMaterial** in the `Assets/GoogleARCore/HelloARExample/Materials/Andy` folder. Ensure that the **Shader** is set to `ARCore/DiffuseWithLightEstimation`. Switch it back if you changed it.
3. Click on the Gear icon and from the context menu, select **Edit Shader**. This will open the shader in your code editor, and it is also shown here for reference:

```
Shader "ARCore/DiffuseWithLightEstimation"
{
    Properties
    {
        _MainTex ("Base (RGB)", 2D) = "white" {}
    }

    SubShader
    {
        Tags { "RenderType"="Opaque" }
        LOD 150

        CGPROGRAM
        #pragma surface surf Lambert noforwardadd
finalcolor:lightEstimation
```

```
      sampler2D _MainTex;
      fixed _GlobalLightEstimation;

      struct Input
      {
          float2 uv_MainTex;
      };

    void lightEstimation(Input IN, SurfaceOutput o, inout fixed4
                         color)
    {
        color *= _GlobalLightEstimation;
    }

    void surf (Input IN, inout SurfaceOutput o)
    {
        fixed4 c = tex2D(_MainTex, IN.uv_MainTex);
        o.Albedo = c.rgb;
        o.Alpha = c.a;
    }
    ENDCG
  }

    Fallback "Mobile/VertexLit"
}
```

4. This is a fairly simple diffuse lighting shader that uses the global light estimate we calculated earlier. It starts by defining itself with this line:

```
Shader "ARCore/DiffuseWithLightEstimation"
```

5. Next, it defines `Properties` in the next code block, where `_MainTex` represents the base texture, is called `"Base (RGB)"`, and is set to `2D`. If you quickly look back at Unity, you can see this property in the **Inspector** window.

6. The block of code that starts with `SubShader` is where the action happens. We first define `Tags`, which are sets of key/value pairs that set the rendering order and type parameters. In our example, we set this to `Opaque`. Then, we have the following line:

```
LOD 150
```

7. This determines the **level of detail** of the shader. The LOD directive is used to determine the complexity or performance requirements of the shader. You can set the value to anything, but typical values are shown in the following list:

- **VertexLit** kind of shaders = 100
- **Decal**, **Reflective VertexLit** = 150
- **Diffuse** = 200
- **Diffuse Detail**, **Reflective Bumped Unlit**, **Reflective Bumped VertexLit** = 250
- **Bumped**, **Specular** = 300
- **Bumped Specular** = 400
- **Parallax** = 500
- **Parallax Specular** = 600

8. As you can see from the list, the simple shader represents a low level of detail. This means that lower-level hardware should be able to run this shader without any issue. You can set the maximum shader LOD per shader or globally; check the Unity documentation for further details.

9. We start our actual shader code with CGPROGRAM and then define the form of surface shader with the #pragma directive, as shown in the following code:

```
#pragma surface surf Lambert noforwardadd
finalcolor:lightEstimation
```

#pragma surface surfaceFunction lightModel [optionalparams]

10. The first part of the directive, surface, defines this as a surface shader. Then, we see that the surf function name refers to the main surface function. Then comes the lighting model, Lambert in this case. After that, the options are set to noforwardadd, which is just a simple way to limit the number of lights to one. Finally, we use a custom modification function called lightEstimation that is set with finalcolor:lightEstimation.

This shader uses the Lambert lighting model. You can find plenty of examples of what lighting models Unity supports or how to write your own model at https://docs.unity3d.com/Manual/SL-SurfaceShaderLightingExamples.html.

11. Just inside the `#pragma` directive, we see the definition of the shader inputs: `_MainTex`, `_GlobalLightEstimation`, and `struct Input`. If you recall, `_GlobalLightEstimation` is the variable we set inside the `EnvironmentalLight` script to represent our global light.

12. Next, we will jump down a few lines to the `surf` function, as follows:

```
void surf (Input IN, inout SurfaceOutput o)
{
  fixed4 c = tex2D(_MainTex, IN.uv_MainTex);
  o.Albedo = c.rgb;
  o.Alpha = c.a;
  }
```

13. This function simply samples the color from our `_MainTex` using `tex2D` and the input `uv` coordinates. Then, it sets the color (`Albedo`) and `Alpha` from the lookup. This function is called first to determine the color of the surface, and then, its output is passed to the Lambert lighting model, after which the final color is set by the `lightEstimation` function.
    An input marked as `inout` represents a value that can be modified and will automatically be returned.

14. Scroll up a bit to the `lightEstimation` function. Inside this function, the code, shown as follows, modifies the color based on the value that was set for `_GlobalLightEstimation`:

```
color *= _GlobalLightEstimation;
```

15. Multiplying the color by the global light estimation is the same as adjusting the brightness with a dimmer switch.

16. Finally, we complete the shader with `Fallback` and the name of another shader. This sets the fall back or backup shader if the current shader is unable to run. A shader can fail due to compilation errors or hardware limitations.

Now that we have a clear understanding of how the light estimation value we saw generated earlier is used in the shader, we can move to perhaps enhancing our lighting. If you recall, our current light just points straight down, but ideally, we would like to position the light to match the strongest light source. We will look at a simple but effective technique to track and position a light in AR in the next section.

Estimating light direction

Google provides us with a robust solution for estimating the amount of light in an AR scene with ARCore. As we learned, light direction is an equally important part of scene lighting. Google didn't intentionally ignore estimating light direction with ARCore; it's just that that problem is really difficult to do right. However, Google did provide us with just enough tools in ARCore to be able to estimate light direction, providing some simple assumptions. First, we need to assume that our user, for now anyway, will remain in the same room or area. Second, our user will need to look in at least an 180 degree arc across their vision, or more simply put, the user just needs to look around. Third, it works best if the real-world environment is lit from a distant single bright source, such as the sun. Based on those assumptions, we can simply store the direction the user saw the brightest image in and use that to reverse calculate our light direction. This may sound more complex than it is, so hopefully, the following diagram can explain this further:

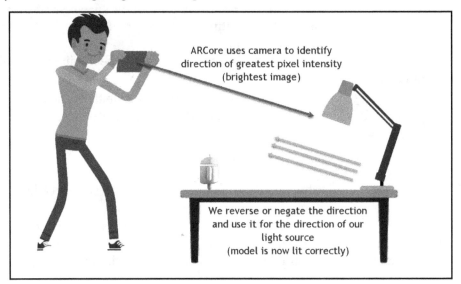

Calculating light direction from camera pixel intensity

Now, this technique may sound quite complicated, but it isn't. We can actually accomplish this with just a few lines of code. Open up Unity and follow along to write our directional light detector:

1. Ensure that the `HelloAR` scene of the sample app is loaded.
2. Select the **Environmental Light** object in the **Hierarchy** window.

3. Click on the Gear icon beside the **Environmental Light (Script)** component in the **Inspector** window and select **Edit Script** from the context menu.

4. Just beneath the class declaration, add the following lines to declare new variables:

```
public class EnvironmentalLight : MonoBehaviour
{  //after me
   public GameObject SceneCamera;
   public GameObject SceneLight;
   private float maxGlobal = float.MinValue;
   private Vector3 maxLightDirection;
```

5. These variables will hold a reference to the scene camera, light, the max global intensity we find, and the direction we find it.

6. Scroll down in the code until you see the identified line in the `Update` method, and add the following lines:

```
const float Inclination = 0.4f; //after me

var pi = Frame.LightEstimate.PixelIntensity;
if(pi > maxGlobal)
{
  maxGlobal = pi;
  SceneLight.transform.rotation = Quaternion.LookRotation(-
SceneCamera.transform.forward);
}
```

7. All this code does is use `Frame.LightEstimate.PixelIntensity` to read the light intensity for the current camera direction. Then, we check whether this value is higher than any previous seen value (`maxGlobal`). If it is, we set a new maximum value and rotate the light (`SceneLight`) in the opposite direction of the camera, which means that the light will face toward the camera.

Be careful when you edit code outside of the `#if UNITY_EDITOR` directive. This code won't be compiled until a build is run for the platform, which means that any errors in the code will be identified as build errors. This can be confusing, so be careful to avoid syntax errors when coding these sections.

8. Save the file; that's all the code we need to write in order to adjust the light direction. If you recall from the last section, the diffuse shader we are using doesn't account for light direction. However, ARCore has provided us with another shader that does.

9. Return to the editor to find and select the **AndyMaterial** in the **Assets/GoogleARCore/HelloARExample/Materials/Andy** folder.

10. Change the material to use the `ARCore/SpecularWithLightEstimation` shader. This material shows the direction of light better.

11. Select the **Environmental Light** object in the **Hierarchy** window. Note how we have two new properties added to the **Environmental Light (Script)** component. These new properties (**Scene Camera** and **Scene Light**) were added because we declared them as **public** fields in the class.

12. Click on the icon that resembles a bullseye next to the **Scene Camera** property. Then, as shown in the following excerpt, select the **First Person Camera** object from the **Select GameObject** dialog:

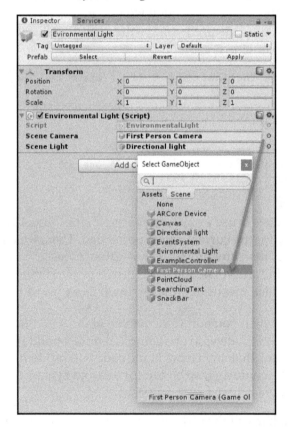

Setting the Scene Camera and Scene Light properties of the component

13. Close the **Select GameObject** dialog.
14. Repeat the same process for setting the **Directional Light** as the **Scene Light**.
15. Connect your device and build and run. Run the app in an area with a single bright light source and see how **Andy** looks after you place it.

Updating the environmental lighting

Now **Andy** should be lit from what looks like the brightest light source in the area. However, because we don't currently track changes in light direction, if you change rooms or the lighting changes, then the illusion is broken. Light tracking is difficult, and it's more difficult than tracking a user, except that we can put a simple hack in place to not track the lighting for as long as we do, which is currently forever, if you weren't paying attention. Follow along to put this simple hack in the code we just wrote:

1. Open up the `EnvironmentalLight.cs` script in your text editor of choice. If you forgot how to do this, just look back a few pages.
2. Add the following line right after and before the lines identified:

```
var pi = Frame.LightEstimate.PixelIntensity; //after me
maxGlobal *= .98f;
if(pi > maxGlobal){   //before me
```

3. That single line is a degrade function on the `maxGlobal` variable. Remember that `maxGlobal` is the value we identify as the strongest light source. This simple function, yep function, degrades this value over time. The value of `.98f` sets the speed of decay. A value of `.98f` represents a fairly quick decay rate, whereas a value of `.9999f` would represent a slow decay.
4. Save the file, and yep, that's it.
5. Go back to Unity. Connect and build and run the app. Now when you place an **Andy**, you should quickly see changes in what the app identifies as the strongest light source. Feel free to go back and change the decay rate or alter the function and use your own method; experiment.

What we put together is a simple way to track and estimate light direction. As we mentioned, this method works, but it's certainly not without its limitations. In any case, this should give the curious reader enough to continue and extend this further. We also completely avoided a proper discussion of shadows. Fortunately, we will have plenty of time to do that in Chapter 9, *Blending Light for Architectural Design*, where we will allow the user to transform their own living space.

Exercises

Complete the following exercises on your own:

1. Change the maxGlobal rate of decay. You decide whether to make it faster or slower.
2. Increase or decrease the maxGlobal rate of decay based on the user's amount of movement. Hint—recall how we tracked the user, and use that to determine how far they have gone or how fast. Use that information to set the rate of decay.
3. Write your own custom lighting surface shader. This one's difficult, but it's worth the effort.

Summary

Certainly, as you become more of an expert in AR, you realize how important lighting is to augmented reality. It's so important that Google developed ARCore with light estimation built in, which is why we spent this entire chapter on the subject. First, we learned about the rendering process in a bit more depth; then, we covered 3D lighting, an essential bit of knowledge that we will need in order to understand the added complexity of lighting in AR. This led us to look at the way ARCore estimates the light levels or global light in an area by taking a closer look at Unity Cg/HLSL shaders and, more specifically, surface shaders. Finally, we implemented a simple but effective hack to track and estimate light direct in a scene, which we left the reader with to improve on in their own time.

Estimating the actual lighting conditions of the environment will be a major hurdle for AR to overcome. However, with the incredible advances in AI and Machine Learning, we will likely see some better solutions come out soon. We will take a closer look at how Machine Learning can assist AR in the next chapter.

Recognizing the Environment 8

Throughout this book, we have looked at the numerous ways of how our device, with the help of ARCore, can track the user, understand the user's world, and render an alternate reality. ARCore uses the device's sensors and camera as inputs to constantly update what it perceives as the user's real world. However, what if we wanted to do more for the user; perhaps identify a certain object, sign, or landmark? That would require a much more advanced set of tools. Even just 5 years ago, this would seem like an incredibly daunting task. With the advent of OpenAI, thanks to Mr. Musk, many other companies have started to open source and make their tools available. This has led to phenomenal explosive growth in these technologies, colloquially referred to as **Machine Learning** (**ML**), and broadened their accessibility to everyone. Fortunately, for those interested in developing AR apps, this is a good thing. We want all the help we can get when it comes to recognizing and understanding the user's environment.

For this chapter, we will introduce ML and explore how we can use it to create better AR apps for our users. In this chapter, we will cover the following topics:

- Introduction to ML
- Deep reinforcement learning
- Programming a neural network
- Training a neural network
- TensorFlow

Machine Learning is a very advanced subject that can take years of study in order to master. However, for our purposes, we will learn some basic techniques, which the reader can extend on later, either through more learning or implementing their own solution.

 If you already have an in-depth understanding of neural networks, convolutional neural networks, and TensorFlow, feel free to breeze over this chapter.

Introduction to ML

Machine Learning is a term widely used to refer to artificial intelligence and related computer predictive analytical models. The name Machine Learning, while perhaps overly generalized, fits better than the term AI. However, Machine Learning is itself such a broad term that it perhaps needs some further explanation and clarification. A machine obviously refers to a computer, or other device and learning tends to denote an algorithm or model that will evolve or learn over time. However, this is often not the case in many Machine Learning models. Therefore, for our purposes, we will use the broader term of Machine Learning to refer to any tool or algorithm that can be trained to recognize the environment or parts of the environment in AR, thus allowing us, the developers, to better augment our user's world.

 Data science and Machine Learning go hand in hand. Data science is all about making sense of data, extracting patterns, and making predictions. In essence, when you start writing Machine Learning models in order to recognize objects or the environment, you are really just analyzing data, which means you can also, very loosely, call yourself a data scientist.

Machine Learning is a big area and is only getting bigger every day, so let's break down the specific problems we would like ML to help us with:

- **Target detection**: Targets have been used in AR for some time. It has been the primary tracking and reference point for many AR apps previous to ARCore.
- **Image recognition**: This spawns into a whole set of sub-applications, all of which we will deal with in detail later.
- **Object detection**: Being able to detect an object in 3D from point cloud data is no easy feat, but it has been done and is getting better.
- **Face detection**: Detecting a person's face in an image has been around for years and has been used to great effect in many apps.
- **Person detection**: Detecting people or motion has great possibilities. Think Kinect comes to AR.
- **Hand/Gesture detection**: Not to be confused with touch gestures. This is where we detect a user's hand motions or gestures in front of a device's camera.
- **Pose detection on object**: Related to object detection, but now we also detect the position and orientation of the object.
- **Light source detection**: Being able to place realistic lights in a scene to make virtual object rendering more realistic. We already looked at the importance of lighting in `Chapter 7`, *Light Estimation*.

- **Environment detection**: Recognizing the environment a user has moved into has great application in mapping buildings or other locations where GPS is unavailable, which applies to most internal spaces.

Each of those problems may require different tools and techniques to solve those issues. In ML, it's not always about using the tool but the final answer and what works. Think about this as you build any ML you need for your app. Try a variety of ML tools and techniques; differences in size and performance of ML models can be critical, and it's something you need to consider.

A Machine Learning algorithm walks into a restaurant.
The waiter asks, "What will you have?
The algorithm says, "What's everyone else having?"

- Unknown

In the following table is a summary of the current major ML providers and the types of AR problems they can be used to solve:

Toolset	Pros/Cons	Machine Learning task						
		Targets/Image	Object/Pose	Face	Person	Hand	Light	Environment
Vuforia	Mature and easy to use. Requires internet connectivity.	Yes	Yes/Paid					
XZIMG	Face and image/target tracking supported for Unity and other platforms.	Yes		Yes				
ARToolkit	Mature OpenSource platform for image tacking and feature detection.	Yes						

EasyAR	Pro license gets object and feature tracking.	Yes	Yes/Paid					
Google Face Detection API	Low level Android API.			Yes				
OpenCV	A mature low-level API for Android, commercial version ported to Unity. Still requires low level knowledge.	Yes	Yes	Yes	Yes	Yes	Coming	Coming
Google TensorFlow	Still in its infancy but quickly becoming the platform standard for CNN. Low level and advanced ML knowledge required.	Yes	Yes	Yes	Yes	Yes	coming	coming
Google ARCore	Currently, identifies planes, feature points, and light.					Yes	Yes	

We only included the main players who have built an AR platform for a mobile ARCore-supported device. Web technologies were omitted from this due to their limitations, although many of the mentioned technologies require internet connectivity and support web platforms as well. If you quickly review the table, you can also clearly see two main contenders that have the potential to dominate the entire space; that's because these are both low-level technologies that often back larger platforms such as Vuforia. Both of these platforms now support mobile pretrained networks for fast recognition on mobile devices. This may not seem like a big deal yet, but after we get into training our own models, you will see why.

Linear regression explained

Let's discuss the basic premise behind what Machine Learning is and what it attempts to accomplish. Take a look at the following chart that shows some fictional sales data for your next app:

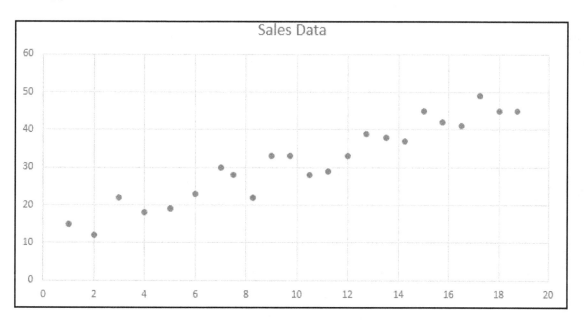

Chart of fictional sales data

Now, just looking at the chart, you can see that as the x values increase (perhaps days on sale), it appears that our sales also increase: y value (sales). By just eyeing the chart, we ourselves can make predictions by following the trend of the points. Try it; how many sales are for an x value (bottom axis) of 25? Give it a guess, and write it down. With your guess secured, we will use a technique called **linear regression** to find a good answer.

Linear regression has been around for years and is considered as the base for many statistical data analysis methods. It is the basis for many other Machine Learning algorithms used in data science and predictive analysis today. This technique works by finding a solution (a line, curve, or whatever) that best fits the points. From that solution, we can determine the future or previous events or occurrences. Since this method is so well established, you can just open up Excel and let it draw the linear regression solution right on the graph. The following is an example of the linear regression with a trend line and equation added to the chart:

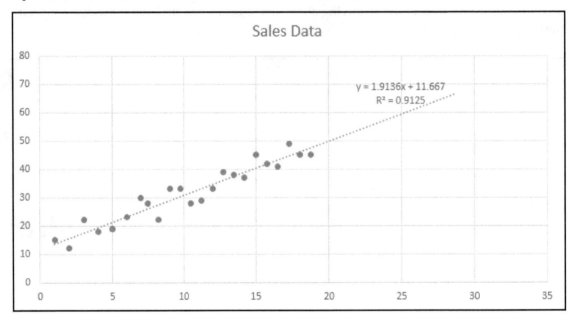

Chart with linear regression trend line

TIP

Keep in mind that this example uses 2D points, but the same concepts equally apply to 3D as well. You just need to account for the extra dimension, which is not always a trivial thing but doable nonetheless.

Without getting into the nitty-gritty details of the math, just understand that the line is drawn in order to minimize the error between the line and the points, which is often referred to as the line of best fit or one that minimizes the error, which in this case, is expressed as an R squared value (R^2). R^2 ranges in value from 1.0, a best possible fit, to 0.0, or shooting blanks in the dark. You can see that our R^2 is not perfect, but it is **0.9125** out of 1 or 91.25% correct; it's not perfect but perhaps good enough.

> Probability and statistics play heavily into Machine Learning of all forms. If you don't have a good statistics background, you can still get the statistics by choosing a third-party provider. The only exception is if you have issues with that technology; then, it helps to have some background on your side, which is probably not something you wanted to hear if you're already trying to catch up on your 3D math skills.

Take the example we just looked at and now think about the problem in 3D, and it's not a line but a 3D object we want to recognize or predict. Obviously, things can get complicated quite fast and computationally expensive using statistical models. Fortunately, there is a better way to do this using a technique that uses **supervised learning** that models the human brain, called **neural networks** (**NN**).

In the next section, we will go under the covers into supervised learning and explore some techniques that we can use to analyze data using **deep learning** (**DL**) with neural networks.

Deep learning

As we discussed, the more traditional predictive models such as linear regression don't scale well, because they always need to calculate the whole solution using all the available points or data. These types of techniques or models have no ability to remember, learn, and improve, and they are generally classified as supervised models. This has led to the evolution of more advanced learning models known as **reinforcement learning** (**RL**) techniques for solving ML problems. In fact, deep learning and deep reinforcement learning techniques now outclass statistical methods in performance and accuracy by several orders of magnitude. However, that wasn't always the case, and statistical methods are also improving just as dramatically everyday. It really is an exciting time to be getting into Machine Learning.

The following diagram demonstrates the reinforcement learning process:

Reinforcement learning process

In the diagram, you can see that there is an **Agent** (assume computer) and the **Environment** (game or real world). The **Agent** acts on **Observations** from the **Environment**, and those actions may or may not be based on **Rewards**. An RL system using rewards is known as reinforcement learning. The learning method we will use in this chapter is called supervised learning since we are labeling or training to a specific output class. Unsupervised learning is a class of training that doesn't label data but just uses techniques to classify or group data.

There are three classes of training we typically identify: unsupervised learning, supervised learning, and reinforcement learning. Reinforcement learning uses a rewards-based system on top of supervised or unsupervised systems as an enhancement to learning. RL systems can learn this way with essentially no initial training. AlphaGo Zero, which uses a deep RL model, is currently making the news after being able to beat a trained version of itself from scratch, with no human intervention.

Part of the problem in defining all these ML concepts is that they often get woven together, where one learning algorithm or technique is layered on top of another, perhaps using RL with or without supervision. It is quite common, as we will see, to use multiple different layers of techniques to produce an accurate answer. This layering also has the benefit of being able to try multiple different approaches quickly or swap a technique out for something better later.

Deep learning is the term we use to describe this layering process. DL can be trained using any of the training methods we talked about. In any case, we need to stop talking in generalities and actually look at the DL process.

Deep reinforcement learning has become quite popular as of late with plenty of success from playing Atari games to beating earlier supervised trained versions of itself quickly. If this area of training interests you, ensure that you search for AlphaGo Zero.

Neural networks – the foundation of deep learning

When we speak of DL, we generally think of one ML technique called neural networks. Neural networks were conceptualized by trying to model the human brain. At the core of a neural network is the neuron, called so because it represents a single human brain cell. The following is an image of a human and computer neuron:

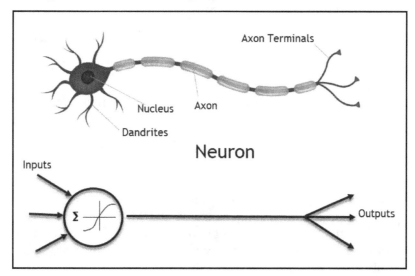

Human and computer neuron

Just like the brain, where billions of neurons are connected in layers, we connect neurons in layers in a similar way. Each neuron is connected to all the other neurons' inputs and outputs in layers, where the first layer takes our input and the last layer or perhaps single neuron spits out our answer. The following is an example of what this typically looks like:

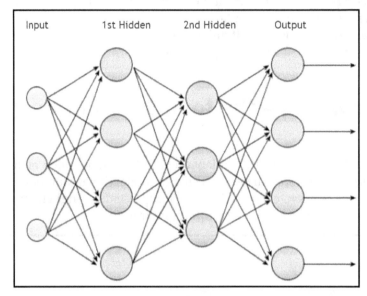

Neural network with layers

 One thing we should clarify before going any further is that the layers we talk about in deep learning don't correspond to the layers in a neural network. Think of a neural network as being in one layer of the DL system.

Here, each circle in the diagram represents a single neuron. Each neuron fires when the sum of all its inputs passes some threshold or activation function. This process continues for all the neurons, and the final layer outputs the answer. Of course, this is a very simple example, but it is difficult to see the power of neural networks until you start programming with them. Therefore, in the next section, we will write a neural network, which we plan to use to recognize objects in the environment.

When you encounter neural networks for the first time, the assumption is that this can't possibly work. After all, how could a self-driving car recognize a person using just a bunch of interconnected neurons? The answer to that is how indeed. We are really only starting to understand how the neural networks do what they do and, often, what we find is that we need to go back to the drawing board. In this case, the drawing board is the human brain and some of the more recent advances in neural networks were results of further brain research.

Programming a neural network

The best way to learn something is to do it, so in this section, we will write a simple neural network that we'll then train to perform various tasks. This network will have a set number of layers—input, hidden, and output—but we will allow for a number of neurons to be set in each layer. We will write this code in Unity so that we can use it in Chapter 10, *Mixing in Mixed Reality*.

 Writing a neural network is an advanced example, which will require a discussion with math to properly explain. If you feel overwhelmed at any time, you can always open up the finished project and check the final results. Of course, if you have written a neural network earlier, then you may also want to skip this section.

For this example, we will create a new project from the source Unity template, so let's get started by opening Command Prompt:

1. Create a new folder called ARCore off the root (C:\ on Windows) folder using the following commands:

```
mkdir ARCore
cd ARCore
```

2. This set of commands creates a new folder and then navigates to it.
3. Execute the following command:

```
git clone https://github.com/google-ar/arcore-unity-sdk.git
ARCoreML
```

4. This pulls the Unity ARCore template from GitHub into a new folder called ARCoreML.

5. Open a new instance of Unity and click on **Open** on the **Project** page. This will open the select project folder dialog. Select the new folder you just pulled the template into, `ARCoreML`, to open the project. Wait as the project opens in the Unity editor.

6. Right-click on (*Ctrl* + Click on Mac) the `Assets` folder in the **Project** window. Select **Create** | **Folder** from the context menu. Name the new folder `Scripts`.

7. Open the `HelloAR` scene from the `Assets/GoogleARCore/Examples/HelloAR` folder by double-clicking on it in the **Project** window.

8. From the menu, select **File** | **Build Settings**. Ensure that **Android** is set for the target platform and the `HelloAR` scene is set as scene 0 in the build.

9. Connect your device and build and run. Just ensure that the example runs as you expected on your device.

Scripting the neural network

With the new project set up, we can now start writing our scripts to build a neural network. Go back to Unity and perform the following steps:

1. Open the `ARCoreML/Scripts` folder and then from the menu, select **Assets** | **Create** | **C# Script**. Name the script as `Neuron` and double-click to open it in your editor of choice.

    The code for this example was originally sourced from `https://github. com/Blueteak/Unity-Neural-Network.git`, which shows an excellent example of a simple and concise neural network with training explicitly developed for Unity. We will modify the original code for our needs, but feel free to check out and contribute to the original source if you are interested. This code is great for learning, but certainly, it's not something you may want to use in production. We will look at options for production-ready neural networks in the section on TensorFlow.

2. Delete all the code, leave the `using` statements, and then add the following:

```
using System.Linq; //add after other using's

public class Neuron
{
    private static readonly System.Random Random = new
System.Random();
    public List<Synapse> InputSynapses;
    public List<Synapse> OutputSynapses;
```

```
public double Bias;
public double BiasDelta;
public double Gradient;
public double Value;
}
```

3. Note how this class does not inherit `MonoBehaviour` and thus will not be a game object, which means we will load this class in another script. Then, we create a placeholder for `Random`; we do this because we are using `System.Random` rather than `Unity.Random`. `Unity.Random` only supports generating a random `float`, but we need the precision of a `double`. The rest are just properties that we will discuss as we get to the relevant code sections.

4. Enter the following after the last property declaration but before the class's ending brace:

```
public static double GetRandom()
{
 return 2 * Random.NextDouble() - 1;
}
```

5. We create this `static` helper method in order to generate `double` random numbers from -1.0 to 1.0. This allows for greater precision and assures that our values are always getting generated around 0. Keeping values close to 0 avoids rounding errors and just generally makes things easier to calculate.

6. Next, enter the following code after the `static` method:

```
public Neuron()
{
  InputSynapses = new List<Synapse>();
  OutputSynapses = new List<Synapse>();
  Bias = GetRandom();
}

public Neuron(IEnumerable<Neuron> inputNeurons) : this()
{
  foreach (var inputNeuron in inputNeurons)
  {
    var synapse = new Synapse(inputNeuron, this);
    inputNeuron.OutputSynapses.Add(synapse);
    InputSynapses.Add(synapse);
  }
}
```

7. Here, we set up a base and single parameter constructors. The base constructor creates a `List<Synapse>` for the input and output connections to the neuron. A `Synapse` represents a connection. The other constructor calls the base (`this`) and takes an `IEnumerable<Neuron>` of neurons that it then connects back to. This way, networks can be built bottom up; we will see how this works when we get to the `NeuralNet` class.

8. Next, we will add the rest of the methods for the `Neuron` class:

```
public virtual double CalculateValue()
{
   return Value = Sigmoid.Output(InputSynapses.Sum(a => a.Weight *
                                 a.InputNeuron.Value) + Bias);
}

public double CalculateError(double target)
{
   return target - Value;
}

public double CalculateGradient(double? target = null)
{
   if (target == null)
     return Gradient = OutputSynapses.Sum(a =>
     a.OutputNeuron.Gradient * a.Weight) *
Sigmoid.Derivative(Value);
     return Gradient = CalculateError(target.Value) *
Sigmoid.Derivative(Value);
}

public void UpdateWeights(double learnRate, double momentum)
{
   var prevDelta = BiasDelta;
   BiasDelta = learnRate * Gradient;
   Bias += BiasDelta + momentum * prevDelta;
   foreach (var synapse in InputSynapses)
   {
     prevDelta = synapse.WeightDelta;
     synapse.WeightDelta = learnRate * Gradient *
synapse.InputNeuron.Value;
     synapse.Weight += synapse.WeightDelta + momentum * prevDelta;
   }
}
```

9. We added four methods here: `CalculateValue`, `CalculateError`, `CalculateGradient`, and `UpdateWeights`. `CalculateValue` is used to determine the neuron's output based on the activation function we defined in `Sigmoid`. We will get to `Sigmoid` shortly. The other methods are used to train the neuron. Training a neuron is something we will cover in the next section.

10. Stay in the same file, and add the following three new helper classes outside the `Neuron` class:

```
} // end of Neuron class definition

public class Synapse
{
  public Neuron InputNeuron;
  public Neuron OutputNeuron;
  public double Weight;
  public double WeightDelta;
  public Synapse(Neuron inputNeuron, Neuron outputNeuron)
  {
    InputNeuron = inputNeuron;
    OutputNeuron = outputNeuron;
    Weight = Neuron.GetRandom();
  }
}

public static class Sigmoid
{
  public static double Output(double x)
  {
    return x < -45.0 ? 0.0 : x > 45.0 ? 1.0 : 1.0 / (1.0 +
    Mathf.Exp((float)-x));
  }
  public static double Derivative(double x)
  {
    return x * (1 - x);
  }
}
public class DataSet
{
  public double[] Values;
  public double[] Targets;
  public DataSet(double[] values, double[] targets)
  {
    Values = values;
    Targets = targets;
  }
}
```

11. The first class `Synapse`, as we already know, defines a connection between neurons. Next comes `Sigmoid`, which, conveniently enough, is just a wrapper class for the sigmoid activation function we use. Note that the values are getting capped at −45.0 and +45.0. This limits the size of our network, but we can manually change that later. Then comes `DataSet`, which is just a holder for our training data.

That completes the `Neuron` class. Create another script in Unity, and this time, call it `NeuralNet`; open it up in your editor of choice and perform the following steps:

1. Delete the starter code again, but leave the `using`'s statements, and enter the following:

```
public class NeuralNet
{
    public double LearnRate;
    public double Momentum;
    public List<Neuron> InputLayer;
    public List<Neuron> HiddenLayer;
    public List<Neuron> OutputLayer;

}   //be sure to add ending brace
```

2. Again, this is another set of public properties that define the `LearnRate` network and `Momentum`. Then, three `List<Neuron>` to hold the collection of neurons in the input, hidden (middle), and output layers. In this example, we use a single hidden layer, but more sophisticated networks often support several more layers. You guessed it, `LearnRate` and `Momentum` will be covered in the section on training.

 We generally prefer not to use properties with getters and setters in Unity. Why? Primarily because the Unity editor just plays better with public fields. Secondarily, game programming is all about performance, and it only makes sense to avoid the overhead of getters and setters where possible. Using a list is also a no-no, but it makes the code easier to understand in this case.

3. Next, let's add a constructor for our `NeuralNet`:

```
public NeuralNet(int inputSize, int hiddenSize, int outputSize,
            double? learnRate = null, double? momentum = null)
{
    LearnRate = learnRate ?? .4;
    Momentum = momentum ?? .9;
```

```
      InputLayer = new List<Neuron>();
      HiddenLayer = new List<Neuron>();
      OutputLayer = new List<Neuron>();
      for (var i = 0; i < inputSize; i++){
        InputLayer.Add(new Neuron());
      }
      for (var i = 0; i < hiddenSize; i++){
        HiddenLayer.Add(new Neuron(InputLayer));
      }

      for (var i = 0; i < outputSize; i++){
        OutputLayer.Add(new Neuron(HiddenLayer));
      }
    }
```

4. This constructor expects several inputs, including the number of neurons in the input, hidden, and output layers, in addition to a value for the `learnRate` and `momentum`. Inside the constructor, the properties are initialized based on the input values. Note how the first layer uses the default `Neuron` constructor, and the successive layers use the single parameter constructor with the previous layer as input. Remember from building the `Neuron` class that this is where all the synapse connections between the neuron layers are added.

5. Next, we will add a couple of methods for training:

```
    public void Train(List<DataSet> dataSets, int numEpochs)
    {
      for (var i = 0; i < numEpochs; i++)
      {
        foreach (var dataSet in dataSets)
        {
          ForwardPropagate(dataSet.Values);
          BackPropagate(dataSet.Targets);
        }
      }
    }

    public void Train(List<DataSet> dataSets, double minimumError)
    {
      var error = 1.0;
      var numEpochs = 0;
      while (error > minimumError && numEpochs < int.MaxValue)
      {
        var errors = new List<double>();
        foreach (var dataSet in dataSets)
        {
          ForwardPropagate(dataSet.Values);
```

```
      BackPropagate(dataSet.Targets);
      errors.Add(CalculateError(dataSet.Targets));
    }
    error = errors.Average();
    numEpochs++;
  }
}
```

6. Then, we will add methods to propagate the network forward and backward:

```
private void ForwardPropagate(params double[] inputs)
{
  var i = 0;
  InputLayer.ForEach(a => a.Value = inputs[i++]);
  HiddenLayer.ForEach(a => a.CalculateValue());
  OutputLayer.ForEach(a => a.CalculateValue());
}

private void BackPropagate(params double[] targets)
{
  var i = 0;
  OutputLayer.ForEach(a => a.CalculateGradient(targets[i++]));
  HiddenLayer.ForEach(a => a.CalculateGradient());
  HiddenLayer.ForEach(a => a.UpdateWeights(LearnRate, Momentum));
  OutputLayer.ForEach(a => a.UpdateWeights(LearnRate, Momentum));
}
```

7. Finally, add the following methods to compute the whole network and to calculate errors:

```
public double[] Compute(params double[] inputs)
{
  ForwardPropagate(inputs);
  return OutputLayer.Select(a => a.Value).ToArray();
}

private double CalculateError(params double[] targets)
{
  var i = 0;
  return OutputLayer.Sum(a =>
Mathf.Abs((float)a.CalculateError(targets[i++])));
}
```

That completes the neural network code. We left a number of areas for discussion in the next section on training the neural network.

Training a neural network

As you may have already summarized, a neural network is essentially useless until it is trained. Before we get into training, we should talk some more on how a neuron is activated. Open up the `Neuron` class again and take a look at the `CalculateValue` function. This method calculates the output based on its internal set of weights and is described by the following:

$$\sum_{i=0}^{n} = w_i * I$$

$$O = S(\sum_{i=0}^{n} w_i \times I) + b$$

Here:

$$S(x) = 1 \div (1 + e^{-x})$$

Also, keep the following in mind:

n = total number of neurons connected as inputs
I = signaled input to the `Neuron` class

O = calculated output

S = the `sigmoid` function with a graph:

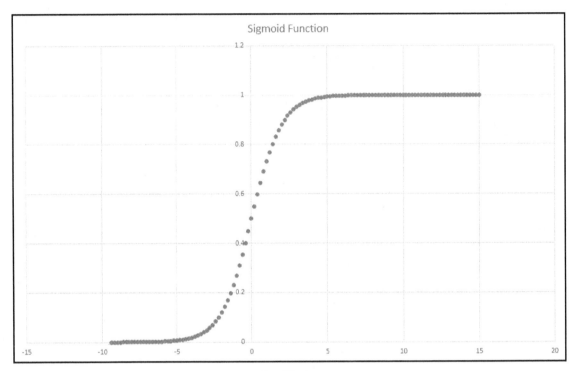

Sigmoid function

Sigmoid Function essentially distributes the weighted sum of values between **0** and **1** based on a curve (function) similar to the one shown in the preceding graph. We do this in order to evenly weigh the outputs of each of the neurons. Likewise, when we look to input data into a network, we also like to normalize the values between **0** and **1**. If we didn't do this, one single neuron or input could bias our entire network. This is like hitting your thumb with a hammer and only being able to feel pain in your thumb for the next several seconds, Except that we don't want our network to respond to wild inputs like that. Instead, we want to mellow our network out with the `sigmoid` function.

Activating the warning

Let's delay our discussion of training a bit further and put together a simple example to see how this works. Open up Unity again and perform the following steps:

1. Create a new C# script called `EnvironmentScanner` in the `Assets/ARCoreML/Scripts` folder. Then, open the script in your editor.

2. Add the code, as shown, to the class definition:

```
[RequireComponent(typeof(AudioSource))]
public class EnvironmentalScanner : MonoBehaviour  //before me
```

3. `RequireComponent` is a custom Unity attribute that forces a `GameObject` to require a specific class before this component can be added. In this example, we require an `AudioSource` component.

4. Enter the following new properties/fields and method to the class; don't delete anything:

```
public NeuralNet net;
public List<DataSet> dataSets;
private float min = float.MaxValue;
private float maxRange = float.MinValue;
private float[] inputs;
private double[] output;
private double temp;
private bool warning;
private AudioSource audioSource;
private double lastTimestamp;

public void Awake()
{
    int numInputs, numHiddenLayers, numOutputs;
    numInputs = 1; numHiddenLayers = 4; numOutputs = 1;
    net = new NeuralNet(numInputs, numHiddenLayers, numOutputs);
    dataSets = new List<DataSet>();
}
```

5. The `Awake` method is special in Unity in that it gets called when the object first wakes up or becomes active. `Awake` varies from `Start` in that it is called upon initialization of the object, whereas `Start` is called before the first frame an object is rendered. The difference is subtle and is typically only relevant when you are worried about object load time.

   Next, we create a number of temporary input variables for setting the number of **input**, **hidden**, and **output** neurons. For this example, we will use one input, four hidden, and one output. These inputs are used to create `NeuralNet` in the next line, which is followed by the initialization of the `dataSets` list.

6. Next, let's modify the `Start` method to resemble the following:

```
void Start()
{
    dataSets.Add(new DataSet(new double[]{ 1,.1,0.0}, new double[] {
0.0,1.0,1.0 } ));
    net.Train(dataSets, .001);
    audioSource = GetComponent<AudioSource>();
}
```

7. The first line inside `Start` creates a very simple `DataSet` with inputs and outputs. Since we are using a single input and output neuron, these inputs and outputs map **1** to **1** and thus produce the following chart:

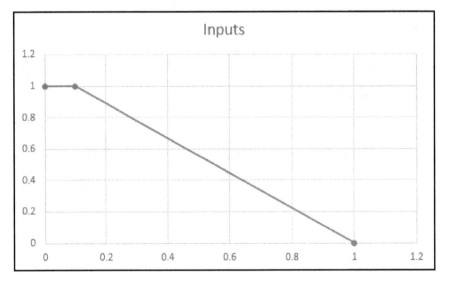

Chart of training inputs

8. Then, `net.Train` trains the neural network with a minimum error of `.001`. After that, it gets the required `AudioSource`, remembers the `RequireComponent` attribute, and sets it to a private `audioSource` field. We will use sound in order to warn the user when they get too close. Think about what it is that those points are describing as a function.

9. Finally, modify the `Update` method to include the following:

```
void Update()
{
  if (warning)
  {
    audioSource.Play();
  }
  else
  {
    audioSource.Stop();
  }
  // Do not update if ARCore is not tracking.
  if (Frame.TrackingState != FrameTrackingState.Tracking)
  {
    return;
  }
  min = float.MaxValue;
  PointCloud pointCloud = Frame.PointCloud;
  if (pointCloud.PointCount > 0 && pointCloud.Timestamp >
lastTimestamp)
  {
  lastTimestamp = pointCloud.Timestamp;
  //find min
    for (int i = 0; i < pointCloud.PointCount; i++)
    {
      var rng = Mathf.Clamp01((pointCloud.GetPoint(i)-
transform.parent.parent.transform.position).magnitude);
      min = Mathf.Min(rng, min);
    }
    //compute output
    output = net.Compute(new double[] { (double)min });
    if(output.Length > 0)
    {
      warning = output[0] > .001;
    }
    else
    {
      warning = false;
    }
  }
}
```

```
}
```

10. There is a lot going on here, so let's break it down. We first check whether the
    `warning` is `true`. If it is, we play a sound, otherwise we stop playing; `warning`
    will be our flag to indicate when our NN is signalling. Next, we ensure that the
    `Frame` is tracking, with the same code as we saw earlier. Then, we reset `min` and
    get the current point cloud from the `Frame`.

    After that, we ensure that `pointCloud` has points, and it is the most recent. This
    is checked by testing the timestamp. Then, inside the `if` block, we calculate the
    current min by looping through all points. We then push this through our NN
    with `net.Compute`, the value of `min` (minimum point); this returns our signal or
    neuron output. In this particular case, we are testing for `.001` to determine
    whether the neuron is signalling an activation. This sets the warning to `true` or
    `false`.

11. Save the code and return to Unity; ensure that you see no compiler errors.

Adding the environmental scanner

Now that we have a script that uses the component, let's add it to our scene as a new object.
Return to the editor where we last left off and continue as follows:

1. Open the `HelloAR` scene. From the menu, select **File** | **Save as** and save the scene
   as `Main` in the `Assets/ARCoreML` folder.
2. Find and select **First Person Camera** in the **Hierarchy** window. Remember that
   you can use the search panel.
3. Right-click (*Ctrl* + Click on Mac) on the **First Person Camera** and from the context
   menu, select **Create Empty**. Name the object as `Environmental Scanner`.
4. Select the new object and in the **Inspector** window, add a new `AudioSource`
   component.
5. Create a new folder called `Audio` in the `Assets/ARCoreML` path in the **Project**
   window.
6. Open the `Resources` folder from the downloaded code folder and copy the
   `tone-beep.wav` file to the new `Assets/ARCoreML/Audio` folder you just
   created.
7. Open up the `Environmental Scanner` object in the **Inspector** window and set
   the **AudioSource** properties, as shown in the following screenshot:

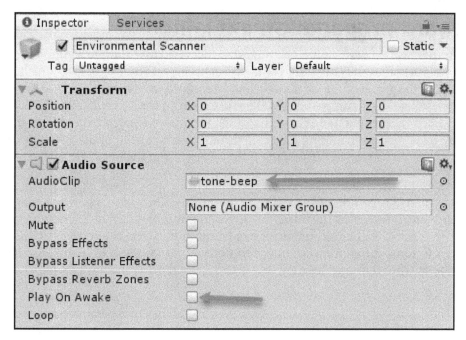

Setting the AudioSource properties in the Inspector

8. With `Environmental Scanner` still selected, click on the **Add Component** button in the **Inspector** window. Add the `Environmental Scanner` script we wrote earlier.

9. Open the **Build Settings** dialog and ensure that you add the current scene (`Main`) to the build. Ensure that you remove any other scenes from the build.

10. Connect, build, and run. Move around the room. Now what happens when you get too close to objects? At what distance?

Great, so we have effectively made a backup or warning beeper to let you know when you are getting too close to an object. Obviously, we could have just as easily written a simple threshold test ourselves to test when `min` is getting too close. However, this simple example gives us a good basis for understanding how training works.

Backward propagation explained

In this example, we are pretraining our model (supervised learning) to a simple function described by a set of inputs (1.0, 0.1, 0) and expected outputs of (0, 1.0, 1.0), which is represented by the graph/chart we saw earlier. In essence, we want our neural net to learn the function defined by those points and be able to output those results. We do this by calling net.Train, passing in datasets and the minimum expected error. This trains the network by backward propagating the error through each neuron of the network until a minimum error can be reached. Then, the training stops and the network declares itself ready.

Backward propagation works using a simple iterative optimization algorithm called **gradient descent**, which uses the minimum error to minimize each of the neuron input weights so that the global minimum error can be reached. To fully understand this, we will need to go into some differential calculus and derivatives. Instead, we will take a shortcut and just look at what the code is doing in the Train method of the NeuralNet class:

```
public void Train(List<DataSet> dataSets, double minimumError)
{
  var error = 1.0;
  var numEpochs = 0;
  while (error > minimumError && numEpochs < int.MaxValue)
  {
    var errors = new List<double>();
    foreach (var dataSet in dataSets)
    {
      ForwardPropagate(dataSet.Values);
      BackPropagate(dataSet.Targets);
      errors.Add(CalculateError(dataSet.Targets));
    }
    error = errors.Average();
    numEpochs++;
  }
}
```

The code here is relatively straightforward. We set an `error` and `numEpochs`. Then, we start a `while` loop that ends when the `error` is greater than the `minimumError` (global) and the `numEpochs` is less than the maximum `int` value. Inside the loop, we then loop through each `dataSet` in `dataSets`. First, `ForwardPropagate` is used on the inputs of the dataset values to determine output. Then, `BackPropagate` is used on the dataset target value to adjust the weights on each of the neurons using gradient descent. Let's take a look inside the `BackPropagate` method:

```
private void BackPropagate(params double[] targets)
{
    var i = 0;
    OutputLayer.ForEach(a => a.CalculateGradient(targets[i++]));
    HiddenLayer.ForEach(a => a.CalculateGradient());
    HiddenLayer.ForEach(a => a.UpdateWeights(LearnRate, Momentum));
    OutputLayer.ForEach(a => a.UpdateWeights(LearnRate, Momentum));
}
```

This method just elegantly loops through each layer of neurons using `ForEach` from `System.Linq`. First, it calculates the gradient in the output and hidden layers and then it adjusts the weights in reverse order: first the hidden and then the output. Next, we will dissect the `CalculateGradient` method:

```
public double CalculateGradient(double? target = null)
{
    if (target == null)
        return Gradient = OutputSynapses.Sum(a => a.OutputNeuron.Gradient *
a.Weight) * Sigmoid.Derivative(Value);

    return Gradient = CalculateError(target.Value) *
Sigmoid.Derivative(Value);
}
```

We can see that the `CalculateGradient` method takes a nullable `double` called `target`. If `target` is `null`, the `Gradient` is calculated by summing the previous gradient multiplied by the input weights. Otherwise, the `Gradient` is calculated by multiplying the error by the derivative of the `Sigmoid`. Remember that, sigmoid was our activation function, which is essentially what we are trying to minimize. If you recall from calculus, we can take the derivative of a function in order to determine its minimum or maximum value. In fact, in order to use the gradient descent method for backward propagation, your activation function has to be differentiable.

Gradient descent explained

Gradient descent uses the partial derivative of the loss or error function in order to propagate the updates back to the neuron weights. Our cost function in this example is the sigmoid function, which relates back to our activation function. In order to find the gradient for the output neuron, we need to derive the partial derivative of the sigmoid function. The following graph shows how the gradient descent method walks down the derivative in order to find the minimum:

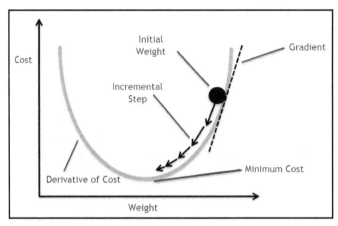

Gradient descent algorithm visualized

 If you plan to spend anymore time studying neural networks, deep learning, or machine learning, you will certainly study the mathematics of gradient descent and backward propagation in more depth. However, it is unlikely that you will get further exposure to the basic concepts of programming a neural network, so this chapter will be a good future reference.

Let's take a look at the `CalculateError` function, which simply subtracts the neuron's output value from what its value should have been:

```
public double CalculateError(double target)
{
    return target - Value;
}
```

Then, scroll to the `UpdateWeights` method, as shown in the following code:

```
public void UpdateWeights(double learnRate, double momentum)
{
    var prevDelta = BiasDelta;
```

```
BiasDelta = learnRate * Gradient;
Bias += BiasDelta + momentum * prevDelta;

foreach (var synapse in InputSynapses)
{
    prevDelta = synapse.WeightDelta;
    synapse.WeightDelta = learnRate * Gradient *
                          synapse.InputNeuron.Value;
    synapse.Weight += synapse.WeightDelta + momentum * prevDelta;
}
}
```

`UpdateWeights` then adjusts each of the neurons' weights based on `learnRate` and `momentum`; `learnRate` and `momentum` set the speed at which the NN will learn. We often want to control the learning rate of the algorithm to prevent overfitting and falling into a local minimum or maximum. After that, the code is relatively straightforward, with it looping through the synapse connections and updating the weights with a new value. The `Bias` is used to control the intercept of the sigmoid activation function, thus allowing the neuron to adjust its initial activation function. We can see how the `Bias` can alter the activation function in the following graph:

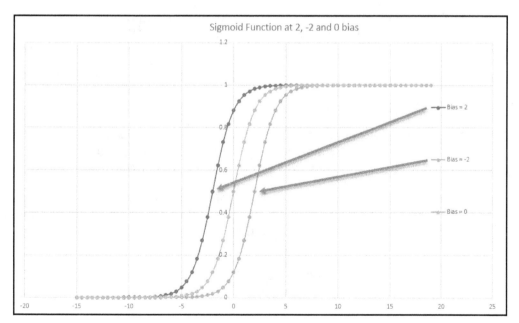

Effect of Bias on the sigmoid activation function

Adjusting the `Bias` allows for the neuron to start firing or activating at a value other than **0**, as indicated in the preceding graph. Thus, if the value of `Bias` is **2**, then the neuron will start activating at **-2**, as shown in the graph.

Defining the network architecture

We just learned how to write and use a simple neural network to warn a user when they are getting too close to an object. As you look through the code, appreciate that most of these values are internally adjusted as part of training. When using a neural network, it is important to understand these basic principals:

- **Activation function**: If you are not using sigmoid, then you will also need to find the partial derivative of your activation function in order to use gradient descent with backward propagation.
- # **Input neurons**: This will not only set the complexity of the network, but it will also determine the number of hidden or middle layer of neurons.
- # **Output neurons**: How many outputs or ways do you need your network to classify?
- # **Hidden layers/neurons**: As a good rule of thumb, you want to use the average of the input and output neurons, or just *input+output/2*. We will apply this rule in our next example.
- **Training method**: Our neural network supports two methods of training: minimum error or by epoch or number of iterations. Our preference will be to use minimum error, as this quantifies our model better.

Included in the source code download for this chapter is a working example in an asset package of our simple neural network being used as an environment or object recognizer. Jump back to Unity and perform the following steps to set up this example:

 Ensure that you save your existing project or download a new ARCore template before beginning. The asset import will overwrite your existing files, so you should make a backup before continuing if you want to keep any of your earlier work.

1. From the menu, select **Assets | Import Package | Custom Package**. Use the file dialog to navigate to the `Code/Chapter_8` folder of the book's downloaded source code and import `Chapter_8_Final.unitypackage`.

2. Open the **Main** scene from the `Assets/ARCoreML` folder.

3. Open the **Build Settings** dialog and ensure that the **Main** scene is added to the build and is active.

4. Connect, build, and run. Now when you run the app, you will see two buttons at the top of the interface: one that says **Train 0** and one that says **Train 1**.

5. Face your device on an area you want the NN to recognize. Ensure that ARCore is identifying plenty of blue points on the screen, and then press the **Train 1** button; this will signal to the network that you want it to identify this feature set.

6. Face the device on an area that you don't want the NN to recognize and press the **Train 0** button; this will reinforce to the network that you do not want it to recognize this area.

7. While staying in place, continue this process. Point your device at the same area you want recognized repeatedly and press **Train 1**. Likewise, do this for areas you don't want recognized, but ensure that you press the **Train 0** button. After you train 10 or so times, you should start hearing the warning beep, identifying when the NN has recognized your area.

8. If you start hearing the warning tones, that will be an indicator that your NN is starting to learn. Continue to spin around in the place, training the network, making sure to correct the network by pressing the appropriate button. You will likely have to do this several times (perhaps 20 to 50 times or so) before you note that the NN recognizes the area you want.

Ensure that when you are training the network, you can see plenty of blue points. If you don't see any points, you will essentially be training with null data.

9. Finally, when your network is fully trained, you should be able to spin slowly around the room and hear when your device recognizes your region of choice.

Using our simple NN, we were able to build an object/feature recognizer that we could train to recognize specific features, places, or objects. This example is quite simple and not very robust or accurate. However, considering the limited training dataset, it does a good job of being able to recognize features on the fly. Open up the `Environmental Scanner` script, and we will take a look at how the network is configured:

1. Scroll down to the `Awake` method and take a look at how the network is created:

```
public void Awake()
{
  int numInputs, numHiddenLayers, numOutputs;
  numInputs = 25; numHiddenLayers = 13; numOutputs = 1;
  net = new NeuralNet(numInputs, numHiddenLayers, numOutputs);
  dataSets = new List<DataSet>();
  normInputs = new double[numInputs];
}
```

2. Note that this time we are creating an input layer of 25 neurons and output of 1. If we stick to the general rule for our hidden layer being the average of the input and output, that equates to 13 [(25+1)/2=13].

3. We removed the initial NN setup and training from `Start` and moved it to the bottom in a new method called `Train`:

```
private void Train()
{
  net.Train(dataSets, 100);
  trained = dataSets.Count > 10;
}
```

4. This time, we are using a different form of training called **epoch**. We use this form of training when we are not actually sure what the expected error is or it needs to change, as in this case. Think about this—when we start training our network with a very limited dataset, our error rates will be high due to our lack of data. This will mean that we will never be able to train our network to a minimum error. It, therefore, makes more sense to just run our training algorithm for a set number of iterations or epochs for every training cycle.

5. Just preceding `Train` is `TrainNetwork`, and it's shown as follows:

```
public void TrainNetwork(float expected)
{
  this.expected = expected;
  training = true;
}
```

6. `TrainNetwork` is a public method that we use to signal to the `Environmental Scanner` to initiate a training cycle with the expected outcome. This allows us to wire up event handlers on the **UI** buttons to call this method with an expected value. When you press **Train 0**, `TrainNetwork` is passed `0.0`, and after the **Train 1** button is pressed, `1.0` is passed.

7. Scroll up to the `Update` method and look at the following section of code:

```
if (training)
{
    dataSets.Add(new DataSet(normInputs, new double[] { expected }));
    training = false;
    Train();
}
```

8. This is the block of code that checks the `training` flag. If it is set, it collects the normalized inputs and adds them to `dataSets` with the expected outcome. We then turn the flag off and call `Train`.

9. Scroll up to the following block of code, and you can see how we are normalizing the training `inputs`:

```
for (int i = 0; i < normInputs.Length; i++)
{
    if (i < pointCloud.PointCount)
    {
        //normalize the inputs
        normInputs[i] = inputs[i] / max;
    }
    else
    {
        normInputs[i] = 0;
    }
}
```

10. Here, we are normalizing the `inputs`. An `input` represents the distance or magnitude between an identified point and the camera (user). Normalizing is scaling or converting your data to values in the range 0 to 1. We do this, in this case, by finding the maximum distance of each point and then using that to divide into all the other inputs. The test in the loop to check whether `i` is less than the `PointCount` is to ensure that we always set a value for each input neuron.

The rest of the code is similar to what we wrote earlier and not worth going over again.

The network view of the world

So what exactly is going on here, what is it that the network is identifying? Essentially, we are flattening our 3D view of the world into a 2D line or curve. A typical example of how this line may look normalized is as follows:

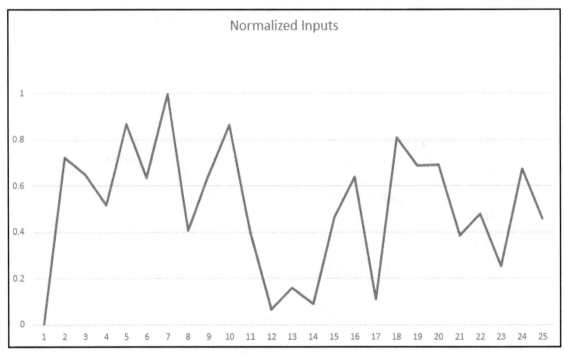

Normalized input points

Those inputs represent the normalized view the neural network is training for, or perhaps, against. If you trained the network to recognize that line, then the warning sound should go off when it detects the said line. Of course, the more points you add, the better your recognizer may or may not work. We will leave it up to you to further test the network on your own.

Neural networks were quite popular with game and graphic developers in the late 1990s and early 2000s. NNs showed some success in various AI scenarios, driving games especially, but at the end, other purpose-built techniques won out, that is, until quite recently with the advent of new techniques such as convolutional NNs. These new successes have led to massive surges in deep learning techniques and platforms.

This simple NN can be extended to recognize other simple functions or patterns you wanted. However, it will work poorly if we try to use it for any of the other recognition tasks we identified earlier as critical for AR. Therefore, in the next section, we will look at how ML solves our recognition problems with a new platform developed by Google, called TensorFlow.

Exercises

Work through the following exercises on your own:

1. Explain the difference between unsupervised learning, supervised learning, and reinforcement learning. This is more of a thought exercise, but it will be beneficial to really understand the difference.
2. Modify the original NN example to warn you when objects are detected past a certain distance.
3. What happens in the second example if you order the inputs by length? Does it still work?
4. Add an additional output neuron to the network in the second example. You will also need a new training button and will need to modify the `TrainNetwork` function to take two `inputs`.

TensorFlow

There is a new kid on the block called **TensorFlow**, also developed by Google, that is making impressive waves in ML. TensorFlow is a full ML platform that is actually more than just an execution engine with a bunch of built-in tools. What is even more impressive is that you can train advanced neural nets, convolutional neural networks, capsule networks, or whatever else you need on massive datasets offline. Then, you take those trained networks and put them on a mobile device in what is called a **MobileNet** to quickly recognize and classify complex objects. We will take a break from ARCore in this section and look at the upcoming power of TensorFlow.

TensorFlow is an advanced ML resource and toolkit that will be worth your time, learning more about whether you need to do any advanced recognition tasks. Keep in mind, though, that this tool requires advanced knowledge in math and a working knowledge of Python.

We will run the TensorFlow example for Android, not just to get a grasp of the power of the tool but also to understand what is possible. With Google building TensorFlow and ARCore though, we can only assume that new integrated tools will be built in the future. For now, though, let's open Command Prompt or shell and get started:

1. Run the following command from your user folder or root:

   ```
   mkdir TensorFlow
   cd TensorFlow
   ```

2. Create the `TensorFlow` directory and navigate to it. Then, type the following command:

   ```
   git clone https://github.com/tensorflow/tensorflow
   ```

3. Open Android Studio. From the **Welcome** screen, select **Open an existing Android Studio project**.

4. Use the dialog and navigate to, select the `TensorFlow/tensorflow/examples/android` folder, and click on **OK**.

5. If it asks you to do a **Gradle Sync**, click on **OK**.

6. Open the `build.gradle` file from the **Project** side panel under the **Gradle Scripts** and set the `nativeBuildSystem` variable to `none`, as shown here:

   ```
   def nativeBuildSystem = 'none'
   ```

7. Connect your device and click on the **Run** button, the green arrow icon on top. Follow any necessary build steps and let the apps push to your device.

8. When the build is completed, Studio will have pushed four apps to your device: **TFClassify**, **TFDetect**, **TFSpeech**, and **TFStylize**. Play around with each of these examples and observe the power of some networks running on your device.

The following is an example of the **TFDetect** app running and correctly classifying a dog and person with very high accuracy:

TFDetect correctly classifying a dog and person

Unfortunately, the components needed to run TensorFlow with ARCore are not quite ready yet, so at the time of writing, we couldn't complete a full example. However, the future of ML for AR apps will most certainly be with TensorFlow or some other third-party solution, piggybacking on top of TensorFlow. Google has years of experience in AI/ML, from developing self-driving cars to the Google Home. It has put those years of knowledge into TensorFlow and made it accessible to the world. You would have to be a fool not to spend any time learning TensorFlow if you plan to build your own ML for object/feature recognition.

We had planned to build an example with a trained MobileNet running in ARCore. Unfortunately, the pieces were not quite ready yet, and it made for a far too complicated example. Right around the time that this book is published, we will likely see more tools developed to make integrating TensorFlow into ARCore easier.

Summary

In this chapter, we took a proverbial dive into the deep end—or the deep learning end—of the pool. We started by talking about the importance of ML and what applications we can use it for in AR. Then, we looked at how ML can use various methods of learning from unsupervised, supervised, and reinforcement learning in order to teach an ML agent to learn. We then looked at a specific example of learning ML algorithms, called neural networks and often referred to as deep learning. This led us to build a simple neural network that you can also use to learn the intricacies of neural networks on your own. NNs are very complex and not very intuitive, and it is helpful to understand their basic structure well. We then trained this network on a very simple dataset to notify the user if they get too close to an object. This led to a further discussion of how NNs train with back propagation using the gradient descent algorithm. After that, we looked at an enhanced example that allows you to train the network to recognize an area or object. Finally, we looked at the current king of ML, TensorFlow, and looked at a quick example of what is possible and what is coming soon.

In the next chapter, we get back to building a practical example with ARCore. We will build a simple design app that lets the user virtually decorate their living space.

9
Blending Light for Architectural Design

This is the first of two chapters where we will build real-world AR apps that you can learn from and show off to friends and family. Unlike in the previous chapters, this time we will build our AR app from nothing. That way, we can learn the specific details needed for incorporating ARCore into a Unity project. We have a lot to cover in this chapter, so let's get started. Listed here is a quick summary of the main topics we will cover:

- Setting up the project
- Placing content
- Building the UI
- Interacting with the virtual
- Lighting and shadows

The premise for our app will be an AR tool for architecture and design. The designing apps are very popular in AR right now and fit very well with the toolkit ARCore provides.

Being able to virtually place objects in or over a real-world object and instantly see how it looks has a tremendous benefit to designers and architects. Now a designer using an AR app can instantly transform a space with their vision. Imagine never having to move a couch 15 times to get it just right, ever again.

Setting up the project

We will use the sample project as a template for creating a new project. At the time of writing, doing an ARCore asset import with the beta version still requires considerable project setup. Ideally, we would like to create a project from scratch, but we will do the next best thing. The next best thing will be to clone the project from GitHub into a new folder of our choice. You can start by opening up Command Prompt and following these steps:

1. Create a new folder off your root or working folder and download the ARCore template by executing the following commands:

```
mkdir ARCore
cd ARCore
git clone https://github.com/google-ar/arcore-unity-sdk.git
ARCoreDesign
```

2. This will create a new folder. Switch to it and download the project template from GitHub.
3. Open up Unity to the project dialog and click on **Open**.
4. Use the folder dialog to find and select the ARCoreDesign folder we just downloaded the code to, as shown in the following excerpt:

Opening the ARCoreDesign project

5. Wait for Unity to load. Ensure that you watch for any compiler errors at the bottom of the editor status bar. If you see them, it means you may have a version conflict or that something's changed. Check your version and try to upgrade or downgrade, as needed.

6. The first thing we will do is organize our folder structure. Create a new folder called `ARCore_Design` in the **Project** window by right-clicking (*Ctrl* + Click on Mac) on the `Assets` folder and selecting **Create** | **Folder** from the context menu.

7. Directly underneath the new folder, add folders for `Scripts`, `Prefabs`, `Scenes`, `Materials`, and `Models`, as illustrated:

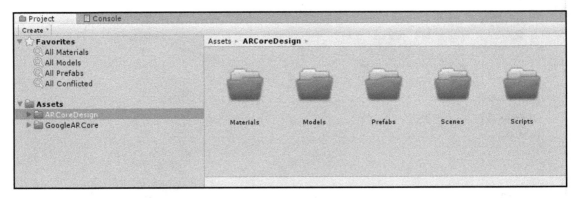

Setting up the folder structure

The technique we just used for setting up the project is useful when you are dealing with other sample projects you want to make your own. Unity manages a project by the folder and the name corresponds to the folder name. We won't worry about setting up source control as you can do this on your own, as you see fit.

If you are setting up this project for anything other than learning, you should definitely consider a source code solution at this point. Dropbox or other file sharing solutions will work in a pinch, but it's not something that will work for more than one developer. There are plenty of free and fairly simple solutions that work with Unity, so take some time and pick one that works for you.

Building the scene

In order for us to save some time, we will load the `HelloAR` scene and modify it to meet our needs. Follow along the given steps:

1. Open the `HelloAR` scene in the `Assets/GoogleARCore/HelloARExample/Scenes` folder by double-clicking on it.

2. From the menu, select **File** | **Save Scene as**, save the scene in the new `Assets/ARCore_Design/Scenes` folder, and name it as `Main`.

Apart from the samples we worked with earlier, from now on, if we need to modify a file, we will copy it to a new appropriate folder, and rename it. This is a good practice to follow when modifying external assets. That way, when you update the asset with a new version, your changes will not be overwritten.

3. From the menu, select **Edit** | **Project Settings** | **Player**.
4. At the **Inspector** window, click on the **Android** tab and edit the **Package Name** to `com.Packt.ARCoreDesign`, as shown in the following screen excerpt:

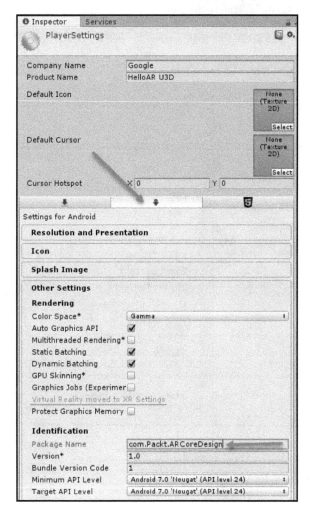

Editing the package name in the Player settings

5. From the menu, select **File | Build Settings**.

6. Click on the checkbox on the `HelloAR` scene to turn it off. Then, click on **Add Open Scenes** to add the new `Main` scene to the build. Ensure that the **Android** option is selected for the **Platform**, and confirm that everything is set, as shown in the following excerpt:

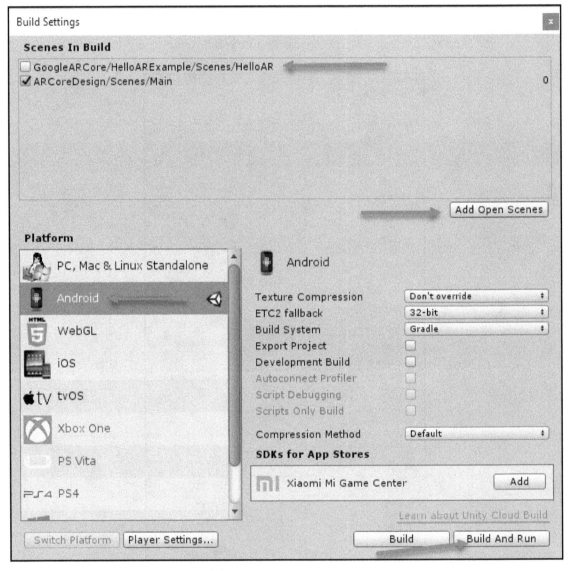

Setting the Build Settings

7. Connect your device and then click on **Build And Run**. You will be prompted to save the APK. Enter the same name you used for the package (`com.Packt.ARCoreDesign`) and click on **Save**. This will kick off the build. A first build can take a while, so grab a beverage or take a quick break.

8. Run the app on your device and confirm that everything runs as you expect it to. If anything fails, refer to `Chapter 11`, *Performance Tips and Troubleshooting*, for help.

 As you work through the exercises in this chapter, try and build as often as possible. A build can quickly tell you if you have any major issues.

Modifying the base scene

The next thing we will do is just modify the base scene for our needs. Open up Unity and follow along:

1. Select and drag the **PointCloud** object in the **Hierarchy** window and drop it into the `Assets/ARCoreDesign/Prefabs` folder in the **Project** window, as shown in the following excerpt:

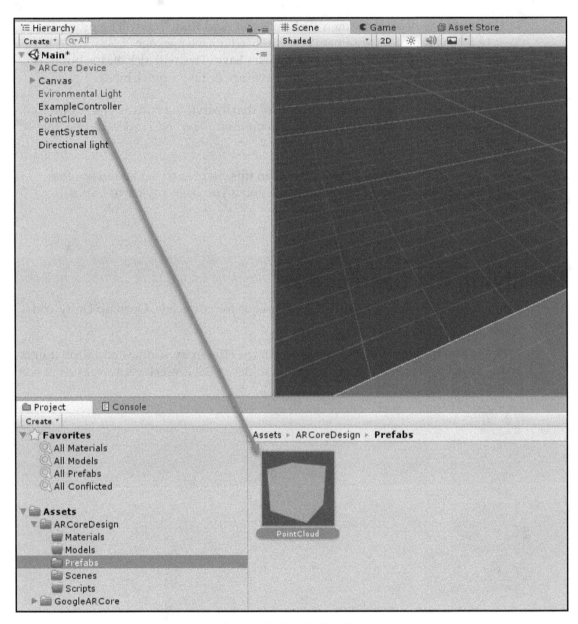

Creating a prefab with the PointCloud object

2. This will create a **Prefab** of the **PointCloud** object. Think of a **Prefab** as a template or almost like a class. Anytime we want to reuse the **PointCloud** object, we can drag it into a scene or instantiate it.

3. Select the **PointCloud** object in the **Hierarchy** window and type the **Delete** key. Find it, and click on it. This will delete the object; we don't need it right now.

4. Rename the `ExampleController` object in the **Hierarchy** window to `SceneController`.

5. Select the `Assets/ARCoreDesign/Scripts` folder and from the menu, select **Assets | Create | C# Script**. Name the script `SceneController`. Then, double-click on it to open the script in your favorite code editor.

6. Now, get back to Unity. Enter `helloarcontroller` in the **Project** search pane to filter the window to the script. Double-click on the script to open it in your code editor.

7. Copy the entire `HelloARController.cs` script and paste it over the contents of the `SceneController.cs` file; yes, all of it. We are essentially making a copy. Rename your class and change the namespace, like this:

```
namespace Packt.ARCoreDesign
{
...   //code omitted
public class SceneController : MonoBehaviour   //rename me
...   //code omitted
}   // don't forget the closing brace at the end
```

8. We wrap all our new code files with a `namespace` in order to avoid naming conflicts. Naming conflicts happen more frequently in Unity if you use a lot of assets. Generally, if you are new to Unity, you will use a lot of third-party assets.

9. Make sure that all the following new `using` statements are identified, as follows:

```
using System.Collections.Generic;
using GoogleARCore;
using UnityEngine;
using UnityEngine.Rendering;
using GoogleARCore.HelloAR;

#if UNITY_EDITOR
    using Input = GoogleARCore.InstantPreviewInput;
#endif
```

10. Save the file and return to Unity. Be sure to watch for any compiler errors.
11. Select the `SceneController` object in the **Hierarchy** window and click on the **Add Component** button in the **Inspector** window.
12. Enter `scene` in the search pane and then select the **Scene Controller** script, as shown in the following excerpt:

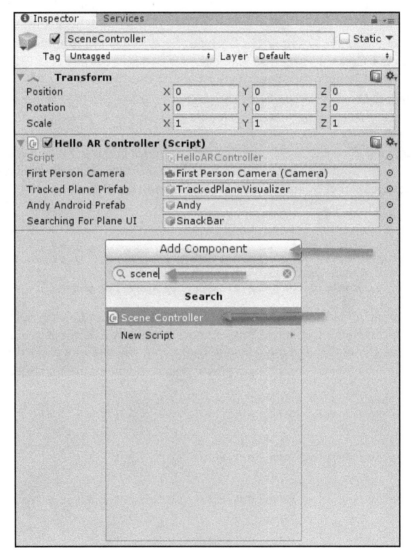

Adding the Scene Controller script as a component

13. Click on the bullseye icon to set the properties for the **Scene Controller**. Ensure that they match **Hello AR Controller (Script)**. When all the properties match, click on the **Gear** icon beside the **Hello AR Controller (Script)** and select **Remove Component** from the context menu. You should now be left with just the **Scene Controller (Scene)** component with the same properties set.
14. Connect, build, and run the app on your device. If you encounter any issues, check for compiler errors and ensure that you set up the components correctly.

We can, of course, create duplicates for all the main scripts, but this will work for now. Obviously, we have a lot more work to do, but this is a good place to start. Ensure that you save the scene and your project. In the next section, we will look to change the content which we allow our user to place and choose where to place.

The environment and placing content

We have already covered the basics of how to interact with the environment in order to place content. What we want to do now is swap out and add new content (sorry Andy). After all, the whole premise of our design app is visualizing in AR how new furniture or other items look in a space. Let's get to it by opening up your favorite web browser and follow along:

1. Browse to `turbosquid.com`. **TurboSquid** is an excellent resource for 3D models, both free and paid.

 For AR / VR and mixed apps, you will generally want your models to be less detailed. Mobile devices such as Android don't render fine detailed models well. Before you purchase any models, ensure that you understand what your device's rendering limitations are.

2. Search for `ligne roset` on the site.

 You can, of course, use any FBX model you like, but try using the one suggested the first time. Working with 3D models can be frustrating if you are unsure what you are doing.

3. Filter your search to free models and select **Ligne Roset Citta sofa and armchair**, as shown:

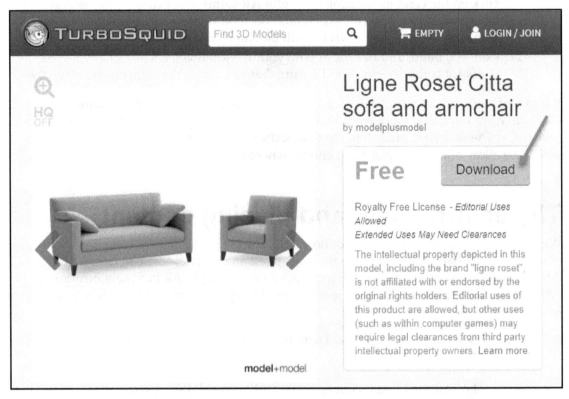

Downloading models from TurboSquid

4. Click on the **Download** button. You may have to create an account and then sign in first.
5. Click on the link marked `Ligne_Roset_Citta_FBX.zip`. This will download the zip file.
6. Unzip the file into a new folder and then open the folder. Select and drag the `mpm_vol.07_p24.FBX` file into Unity and drop it into the `Assets/ARCore/Models` folder, as follows:

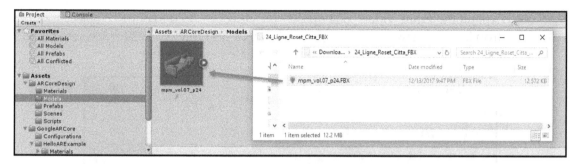

Dragging the model into the Models folder

7. Select the model and then, in the **Inspector** window, confirm that **Model |
Scale Factor** is set correctly, as follows:

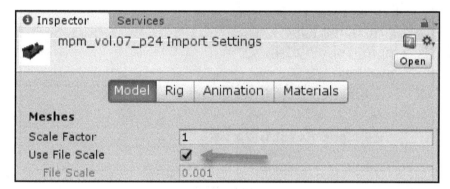

Checking the model scale after import

8. In this example, the model is using **File Scale**, which is set at 0.001. You may
need to adjust this depending on what scale your model uses. Right now, this
scale works.

9. Our model comes complete with chair and sofa. Fortunately, we can break
these apart relatively easily. Drag and drop the model into an open area of the
Hierarchy window. You should see the chair and sofa get added to the scene.

10. Click on an empty area in the **Hierarchy** window again to disable the model
selection.

11. From the menu, select **GameObject | Create Empty**; rename the object as sofa.
Do this again to create another new object and name it armchair. Ensure that the
armchair and sofa game objects are set on an origin pose with a position of
(0, 0, 0) and rotation of (0, 0, 0). If you need help, select the object and check the
Inspector window.

12. Expand the **mpm_vol.07_p24** model, and drag the child `armchair` object and drop it on the new `armchair` game object. Repeat this process for the sofa piece, and your **Hierarchy** window should resemble the following:

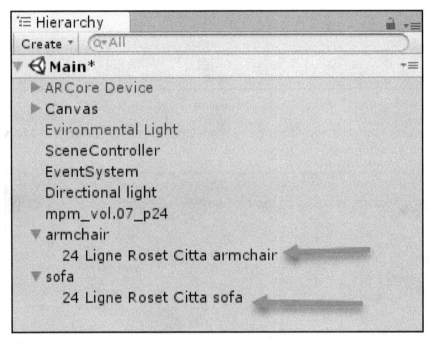

Creating two new models

13. What we just did is create new anchor points and then break apart our model. Anchor points allow us to adjust a model with respect to the fixed anchor. You will often need to do this in cases where the modeling software used a different reference. This is the case with our model. Select the **24 Ligne Roset Citta armchair** child object and check the **Inspector** window.

14. Change the position of the `armchair` **Transform** to (0, 0.25, 0), as illustrated here:

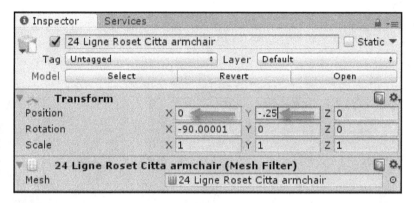

Setting the position transform of the armchair

15. Ensure that the position is set to **X**=0 and **Y**=-.25 and leave the **Rotation** as it is. We are offsetting the position of the `armchair` from where it was and down a little. This is because ARCore currently tends to track planes too high; hopefully, this will be fixed by the time of release. In any case, you can adjust the offset of the position of the `chair` anytime and anyway you want later.

16. Drag the `armchair` object from the **Hierarchy** window and drop it into the `Assets/ARCoreDesign/Prefabs` folder. Repeat this process for the `sofa` object as well. This will create a prefab of the `armchair` and `sofa`.

17. Delete the `armchair`, `sofa`, and original **mpm_vol.07_p24** objects from the **Hierarchy** window.

18. Select the `SceneController` object in the **Hierarchy** window and then in the **Inspector** window, set **Andy Android Prefab** to the `armchair` prefab, as shown in the following excerpt:

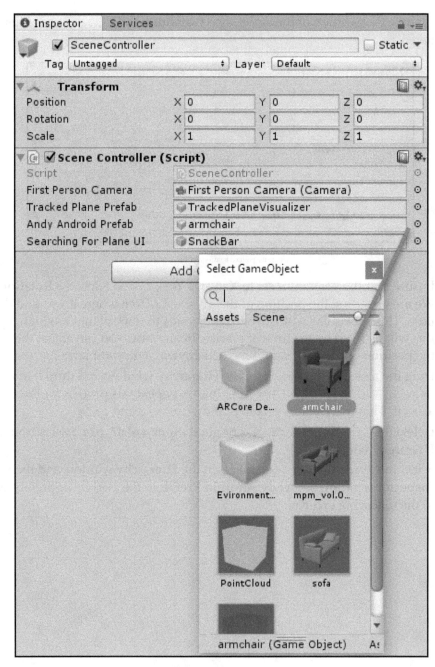

Setting the prefab slot on SceneController

19. Save the project, connect, and run the app on your device. Let some surfaces appear and then place a chair or two. Feel free to go back and swap for the sofa. Note that you may want to adjust the `sofa` model's position as well.

Good, now we can place some furniture, except that you will soon realize that the planes are more in the way now. Let's see how we can turn the planes in the next section on and off when we start adding in some UI.

Building the UI

At this point, we want to give the user the ability to clear a scene and turn off the planes. The planes are helpful to identify surfaces we can drop objects onto, but they really distract from the experience. We will do this by building a dead simple UI with a couple of buttons. Fortunately, Unity has a very powerful UI system called **uGUI**, which will allow us to quickly do this. Open up the Unity editor to the `Main` scene and follow along:

1. Click on an open area of the **Hierarchy** window to ensure that your selection is cleared. We do this to avoid attaching objects to other objects mistakenly.
2. From the menu, select **GameObject | UI | Canvas**. Name the new object as `UI` and ensure that the properties for this object match the **Inspector** window in the following excerpt:

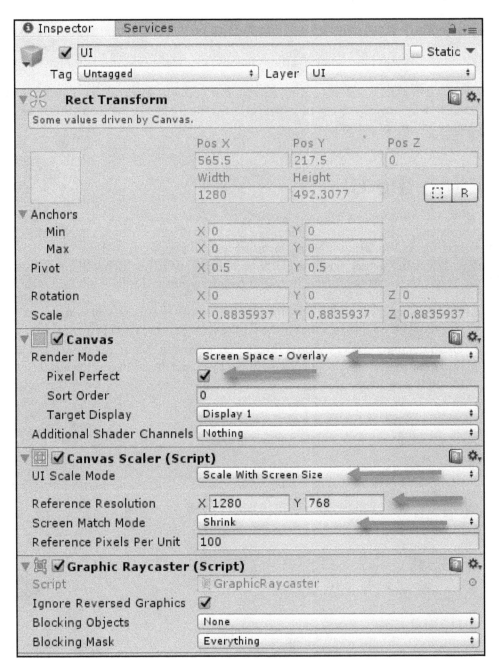

Setting the properties of a new UI canvas

3. The settings we use on this **Canvas** allow our child UI objects to scale automatically with screen size based on a specific resolution. If we didn't do this, our UI controls would scale differently on each device. This allows us to keep a consistent look, which is a good thing.

4. Select the **UI** canvas and from the menu, select **GameObject | UI | Panel** to add a new child panel to the canvas.

5. Select the new **Panel** object. In the **Inspector** window, click on **Add Component** and then search for and add a **Grid Layout Group** component. Then, set the properties of this component to match the following screen excerpt:

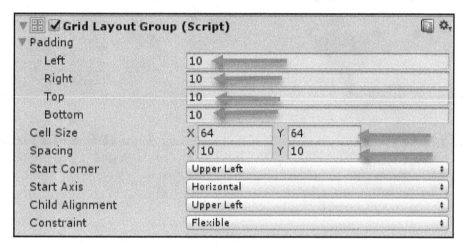

Setting the Group Layout Grid (Script) properties

6. **Grid Layout Group** is a useful tool for automatically laying out objects. The layout will automatically resize itself and adjust its child grid components.

7. With the **Panel** still selected, change the **Image** component's **Color** property to transparent. Do this by clicking on **Color Selector Area** next to the **Color** property and set the color to #FFFFFF00 or Alpha 0.

8. Select the **Panel** object in the **Hierarchy** window and from the menu, select **GameObject | UI | Button**. Rename the button as **Clear**.

9. Expand the **Clear** button and select the child object. Change the **Text** components **Text** property to **Clear**.

10. Repeat the sixth and seventh steps for a new button called **Planes**. When you are done, your **Hierarchy** window and **Game** window should resemble the following excerpt:

The finished buttons and panel in 2D view

11. You can view your scene in 2D view by clicking on the **2D** button at the top of the **Scene** window. This is useful for previewing the **UI** elements you are building. You can use your mouse and keyboard to adjust the view on your own after that.

12. Connect, build, and run. The buttons don't work yet, but change the orientation and see how the buttons scale.

Feel free to style these buttons as you wish; after all, this is your app too. You can also add a slide in menu if you wanted. There are plenty of excellent resources and good books available on Unity uGUI development that can guide you on how to extend the UI for your look and feel.

Scripting the buttons

The obvious next step is to get those buttons working. Of course, we need to add a little bit of scripting, shown as follows:

1. Open the `SceneController` script we created earlier in your code editor. Just before the `Update` method, insert the following section of code:

```
private List<GameObject> m_sceneObjects = new List<GameObject>();
private List<GameObject> m_scenePlanes = new List<GameObject>();
private bool m_planeOnState;
public void ClearScene()
```

```
{
    foreach(var obj in m_sceneObjects)
    {
        Destroy(obj);
    }
    m_sceneObjects.Clear();
}
public void Planes()
{
    m_planeOnState = !m_planeOnState;
    //turn plane visibility on or off
    foreach(var plane in m_scenePlanes)
    {
        plane.SetActive(m_planeOnState);
    }
}
```

2. In this code, we first create some lists to store scene objects (m_sceneObjects) and planes (m_scenePlanes), with a new boolean to track the state of the planes m_planeOnState (visible or not). Next, we add two new methods (ClearScene and Planes). ClearScene iterates over m_sceneObjects using foreach and removes the object from the scene with the Destroy method. Destroy is the method used to remove and clean up game objects from a scene. The Planes method flips the state of m_planeOnState and then loops through the planes and sets their state with SetActive. If an object is active, it means that it is visible and being updated in a scene. An inactive object is disabled and does not render.

 We are staying consistent with the same naming conventions in this example in order to match the code style. If using m_ to denote a private member variable is not your style, don't use it. You may also want to refactor this code and replace names such as andyObject with something more appropriate. Visual Studio has a great set of refactoring tools that make tasks like this easy.

3. Scroll down in the Update method and add the line after the line identified:

```
var andyObject = Instantiate... //after me
m_sceneObjects.Add(andyObject);
```

4. This line of code just adds the andyObject (poorly named now) to our list of scene objects. The andyObject is first instantiated with the Instantiate method. Think of Instantiate as the opposite of Destroy.

5. Scroll back up and add the line after the line identified:

```
GameObject planeObject = Instantiate... //after me
m_scenePlanes.Add(planeObject);
```

6. The same thing here, we are adding the newly instantiated `planeObject` to our list of scene planes.

7. Save the file and return to Unity. We now need to hook up the buttons. As always, wait for the compiler to finish in order to ensure that you didn't create a syntax error.

8. Select the **Clear** button and in the **Inspector** window, scroll to the **Button** component. Click on the + button at the bottom to add a new event handler, and then set the properties of the handler to those shown here:

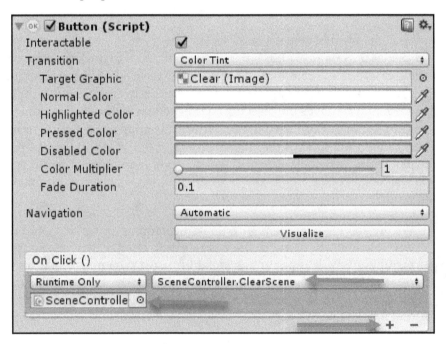

Adding the button event handler

9. Repeat the process for the **Planes** button. This time though, connect the `Planes` method.

10. Connect, build, and run. Try to place an object and then use the buttons to clear it.

Now, you should be able turn on and off the plane visibility and clear any objects you created. In the next section, we will extend our UI to allow the user to interact with the objects.

Interacting with the virtual

We want our users to be able to place and then move or adjust their object's pose as they need to. If you recall, a pose represents the six degrees of freedom that an object can be represented in in 3D space. Before we start posing an object though, we need to be able to select an object. After we select an object, we want to be able to outline it in order to identify it to the user as selected. Since outlining the object sounds like an essential first step, let's tackle that first. Follow along the given steps to create the object outlining:

1. Go back to Unity. Create a new folder in the `Assets/ARCoreDesign/Materials` folder and name it `Shaders`.
2. Right-click (*Ctrl* + Click on Mac) inside the new folder within the **Project** window and from the **Context** menu, select **Create** | **Shader** | **Standard Surface Shader**. Name the new shader `ARMobileSpecularOutline`.
3. Double-click on the `ARMobileSpecularOutline` shader to open it in your code editor.
4. Delete the contents of the file. We will replace it with the ARCore mobile specular shader we used earlier.
5. Open the `MobileSpecularWithLightEstimation.shader` file in your text editor and copy the entire contents to your clipboard. The file is in the `Assets/GoogleARCore/HelloARExample/Materials/Shaders` folder.
6. Paste the contents of your clipboard to the new `ARMobileSpecularOutline.shader` file we just created. Again, we are copying the sample source and converting it to our own.

 While this shader is a copy of our light estimation shader and will use light estimation, we want to try and keep our variable names as succinct as possible. Normally, we will add light estimation to the name of the shader. However, in this, we will use an AR prefix to remind us that this shader uses light estimation and is optimized for AR.

7. Edit the name of the shader, top line, to the following:

```
Shader "ARCoreDesgin/ARMobileSpecularOutline"
```

8. Next, we have several edits to do at the top of the file. Change the **Properties** section to the following by adding the new lines not highlighted:

```
Properties
{
    _Albedo ("Albedo", Color) = (1, 1, 1, 1)
    _Shininess ("Shininess", Range (0.03, 1)) = 0.078125
    _MainTex ("Base (RGB) Gloss (A)", 2D) = "white" {}
    [NoScaleOffset] _BumpMap ("Normalmap", 2D) = "bump" {}
    _Outline ("_Outline", Range(0,0.1)) = 0
    _OutlineColor ("Color", Color) = (1, 1, 1, 1)
}
```

9. This adds three new properties: _Albedo, _Outline, and _OutlineColor. We added _Albedo in order to set a color on our materials without using a texture. _Outline defines the size of the outline, and _OutlineColor refers to the color.

10. After the identified lines, inject the following block of code:

```
Tags { "RenderType"="Opaque" }
LOD 250   //after me
Pass {
    Tags { "RenderType"="Opaque" }
    Cull Front

    CGPROGRAM

    #pragma vertex vert
    #pragma fragment frag
    #include "UnityCG.cginc"

    struct v2f {
        float4 pos : SV_POSITION;
    };
    float _Outline;
    float4 _OutlineColor;

    float4 vert(appdata_base v) : SV_POSITION {
        v2f o;
        o.pos = UnityObjectToClipPos(v.vertex);
        float3 normal = mul((float3x3) UNITY_MATRIX_MV, v.normal);
        normal.x *= UNITY_MATRIX_P[0][0];
        normal.y *= UNITY_MATRIX_P[1][1];
        o.pos.xy += normal.xy * _Outline;
        return o.pos;
    }

    half4 frag(v2f i) : COLOR {
```

```
        return _OutlineColor;
    }

    ENDCG
}
```

11. This block of code is the part that creates the outline and does this by rendering a second time. It does this using the `Pass` keyword. Inside `Pass`, we can see more tags being defined and another start to a shader program with `CGPROGRAM`. The second block is a `vertex/fragment` shader and if you look inside the `vert` function, you can see where the outline is calculated. It does this by projecting the models vertex `normal` a distance determined by `_Outline`. Then, in the `frag` function, we just return the outline color. Again, don't panic if this looks intimidating, it is.

12. The last thing we need to do is add the new `_Albedo` property to our surface shader and add code to use it. Scroll down and add the following line after the identified line:

```
fixed _GlobalLightEstimation;   //after me
float4 _Albedo;
```

13. Scroll down further to the `surf` function and modify the following line:

```
from o.Albedo = tex.rgb;

to o.Albedo = tex.rgb * _Albedo;
```

14. All this is done to apply the `Albedo` color to the texture. If there is no texture, a value of `1.0` is used, which means just the `Albedo` color is shown. We needed to add this bit because our imported models didn't come with textures, and we didn't want to have to use a texture.

15. Save the file and return to Unity. Ensure that you see no compiler errors.

That completes the outline shader, but, of course, we want to test how it works. Let's create a new material and set it on our model to see how this looks:

1. Create a new material called `ARMobileSpecularOutline_Green` in the `Assets/ARCoreDesign/Materials` folder.
2. Change the new material's shader to use the newly created shader **ARCoreDesign | ARMobileSpecularOutline**.
3. Set the `Albedo` color to a pleasant green, perhaps `#09D488FF`. Set the **Shininess** to about `0.5` or so, you decide.

The actual color of the fabric material is `#8F8E2A`; use that color if you don't want such an obvious difference.

4. Set `_Outline` to `0.02`, which is still quite thick, but obvious. Use this value for now, and you can change it later.
5. Select the `sofa` prefab in the `Assets/ARCoreDesign/Prefabs` folder and replace the **fabric** material with the new **ARMobileSpecularOutline_Green**, as shown:

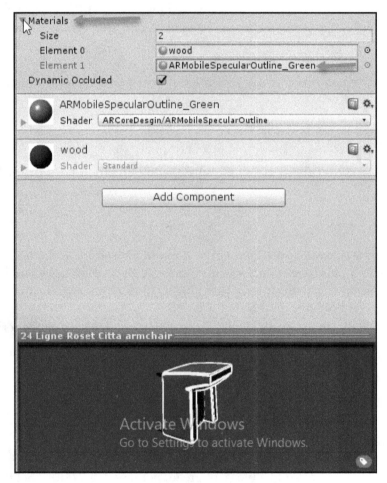

Changing the sofa prefab to use the new material

6. Save your project. Connect, build, and then run. Place a `chair` and see how it looks.

We have our outline shader in place, but now we need to programmatically turn the outline on when a user selects an object.

Building the object outliner

We will build an `ObjectOutliner` class to handle the outlining for us. Follow along as we build the pieces to turn the outline on and off as the user selects an object:

1. Create a new C# script called `ObjectOutliner` in the `Assets/ARCoreDesign/Scripts` folder.

2. Replace all of the pregenerated script with the following:

```
namespace Packt.ARCoreDesign
{
    using System.Collections;
    using System.Collections.Generic;
    using UnityEngine;
    public class ObjectOutliner : MonoBehaviour
    {
        public int MaterialSlot;
        public Material DefaultMaterial;
        public Material OutlineMaterial;
        public bool outlineOn;
        public void Outline()
        {
            outlineOn = !outlineOn;
            var renderer = GetComponent<MeshRenderer>();
            Material[] mats = renderer.materials;
            if (outlineOn)
            {
                mats[MaterialSlot] = OutlineMaterial;
            }
            else
            {
                mats[MaterialSlot] = DefaultMaterial;
            }
            renderer.materials = mats;
        }
    }
}
```

3. This class basically just swaps the material of an object with its outlined or default material every time `Outline` is called.

4. Next, open the `SceneController.cs` script in your code editor. We have to wrap the `Session Raycast` call in the `Update` method with our own `Physics Raycast`. Add the following code around the highlighted code section, as follows:

```
RaycastHit rayHit;
if
(Physics.Raycast(FirstPersonCamera.ScreenPointToRay(touch.position)
, out rayHit, 2))
    {
       var outliner =
rayHit.collider.gameObject.GetComponent<ObjectOutliner>();
       if (outliner != null)
       {
         outliner.Outline();
       }
    }
    else
    {
       // Raycast against the location the player touched to search
for planes.
       TrackableHit hit;
       TrackableHitFlags raycastFilter =
TrackableHitFlags.PlaneWithinPolygon |
       TrackableHitFlags.FeaturePointWithSurfaceNormal;

       if (Frame.Raycast(touch.position.x, touch.position.y,
raycastFilter, out hit))
       {
         var andyObject = Instantiate(AndyAndroidPrefab,
hit.Pose.position, hit.Pose.rotation);
         m_sceneObjects.Add(andyObject);
         // Create an anchor to allow ARCore to track the hitpoint as
understanding of the physical
         // world evolves.
         var anchor = hit.Trackable.CreateAnchor(hit.Pose);

         // Andy should look at the camera but still be flush with the
plane.
         if ((hit.Flags & TrackableHitFlags.PlaneWithinPolygon) !=
TrackableHitFlags.None)
         {
            // Get the camera position and match the y-component with
the hit position.
```

```
        Vector3 cameraPositionSameY =
FirstPersonCamera.transform.position;
        cameraPositionSameY.y = hit.Pose.position.y;

        // Have Andy look toward the camera respecting his "up"
perspective, which may be from ceiling.
        andyObject.transform.LookAt(cameraPositionSameY,
andyObject.transform.up);
      }

        // Make Andy model a child of the anchor.
        andyObject.transform.parent = anchor.transform;
    }/end of Frame.Raycast
  }
```

5. This section of code uses the `Raycast` method of the `Physics` object. `Physics` is the object that encapsulates the Unity physics engine. `Raycast` is a method we use, just like `Frame.Raycast` we saw earlier, to cast a ray and check for any collisions. Normally, you filter out objects to test before you run a ray cast operation, because it is so expensive. You can see how this is done with `Session` in the setup of the `raycastFilter`, where the filter is set to test for planes, but you can also set this point as well. This will allow you to easily apply wall coverings, for instance. In our case, since we are using `Physics` to do the `Raycast`, we can ensure that you only get physics objects. The ARCore planes don't have physics objects attached to them.

6. Save the file and return to Unity.

7. Locate the `armchair` prefab in the `Assets/ARCoreDesign/Prefabs` folder and expand it to see the inner model.

8. Select the armchair model and then, in the **Inspector** window, click on **Add Component**. Add a **Box Collider** to the object; the **Box Collider** will automatically adjust its size to surround the model. The `Physics` engine just tests for collisions against a collider and not the object. This is why we don't have to worry about our ARCore planes and points. If you add other models and want them selectable, then always use the simplest collider that best fits your shape. By simple, we mean less polygons. For instance, don't use a sphere collider when a **Box Collider** will do.

9. Click on the **Add Component** button again and this time, add our new **Object Outliner Script** to the object and set its properties to what is shown in the following excerpt:

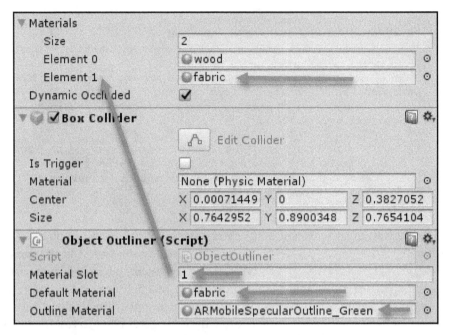

Setting up the Object Outliner properties

10. **Default Material** represents the base look of the model. Then, we set the **Outline Material** to our outline material we created earlier. Lastly, we set the slot we want to replace. The element we want to replace is **Element 1**, so we put 1 in the **Material Slot** property.

11. Save the project, build, and run. Place a chair and then select it.

Now you can place a chair, select it, and then deselect it. If you note that it is difficult to select an object, ensure that you check that the collider is sufficiently large to engulf the object. In our example, the automatically created collider for the armchair is slightly off; perhaps we can fix that issue with one of the exercise questions.

Positioning the chair

The last step is to allow the user to move the chair after they select it. Fortunately, we can do all that in code. Open up your code editor to the `SceneController.cs` file and follow along:

1. Add a new `public` variable to the top of the class after the line identified:

```
public GameObject m_andyAndroidPrefab; //after me
```

```
public float MoveSpeed = .1f;
```

2. This new `float` `MoveSpeed` sets the speed at which the user can move an object. You can also think of it as the move sensitivity. We set it to the default value of `.1f` here, but feel free to change it in the **Inspector** later when testing.

3. Locate the following highlighted section of code and replace it with this:

```
if (Input.touchCount < 1 || (touch = Input.GetTouch(0)).phase !=
TouchPhase.Began)
{
   return;
} //replace me with

if (Input.touchCount < 1) return;
touch = Input.GetTouch(0);
if (touch.phase == TouchPhase.Began) //handle a single touch
{   //starting single touch
```

4. The previous code made sure to only test the for starting touches. Instead, we now want to check when a `touch` starts and then as the user moves their finger. Since our previous `Physics` raycast code wrapped the `Session` raycast code, we now need to wrap it again with code that tests for a first touch and move events, which is what our second `if` statement does.

5. Scroll to the line identified and add the following code before the end of the `Update` method:

```
        // Make Andy model a child of the anchor.
        andyObject.transform.parent = anchor.transform;
   }
} //after me

}   //be sure to add the brace
else if (touch.phase == TouchPhase.Moved)
{
   var change = FirstPersonCamera.transform.forward *
touch.deltaPosition.y;
   change += FirstPersonCamera.transform.right *
touch.deltaPosition.x;
   change *= Time.deltaTime * MoveSpeed;

   foreach (var obj in m_sceneObjects)
   {
     var outliner = obj.GetComponentInChildren<ObjectOutliner>();
     if (outliner != null && outliner.outlineOn)
     {
```

```
        obj.transform.position += change;
      }
    }
  }
```

6. The code we are adding here handles when the user is moving their finger. We then calculate a `change` vector relative to the camera's position. This transforms the `forward` or `z` axis relative to the camera by a delta position of the y axis in 2D, which more or less means that as the user moves their finger up and down on the screen, the object will move in and out on the `forward` axis, relative to the camera. To the `change` vector, we then add the `right` or x axis vector relative to the camera and modified by the delta of the user's finger along the x axis in 2D. Thus, when a user moves their finger left or right across the screen, the model will move left-right along the `right` axis relative to the camera.

7. Scroll up and change the **if** statement to add the new highlighted code starting with **&&**:

```
if (outliner != null && outliner.outlineOn == false)
{
  outliner.Outline();
}
```

8. This change just ensures that if the object is highlighted and selected again, the `Outline` method is not called. We no longer want to toggle the selection, but we will leave the `Outline` method this way for ease of use. Next, we want to handle when a user touches away from an object. In that case, we want to disable all the outlined objects.

   If, at any point, you lose track or get frustrated, take a look at the finished project available as part of the code.

9. Scroll down to the code identified and insert the new code to clear the outlines on the selected objects:

```
else
{  //after me
  //touched outside, reset all outlined objects
  foreach (var obj in m_sceneObjects)
  {
    var outliner = obj.GetComponentInChildren<ObjectOutliner>();
    if (outliner != null && outliner.outlineOn)
    {
      outliner.Outline();
    }
  }
```

```
TrackableHit hit;    //before me
```

10. This code loops through the game `m_scene_Objects`, finds the `ObjectOutliner` component, and then uses that to test whether the outline is on. If the outline is on, it turns it off with a call to `Outline`, perhaps poorly named now.

11. Connect, build, and run. Wait for the surfaces to track and then place a `chair`. Touch to select and then use your finger to move the `chair` around. You can also adjust your position relative to the `chair` and watch how the object responds, all in real time.

12. Press the volume down and power button at the same time to take a screenshot. Compare your picture to the following one:

A virtual armchair placed and moved

Not bad, but we can probably do a bit better. In the next section, we will get back into lighting and work on the lighting and shadows of our objects.

Lighting and shadows

Lighting is an essential element in our scenes, but as we have already seen, it takes some work to get it right. In this section, we will revisit lighting and also tackle adding shadows. Adding shadows to our objects will make them look like they are really there. We will start with adding shadows, so open up Unity and follow along:

1. Create a new shader called `UnlitShadowReceiver` in the `Assets/ARCoreDesign/Materials/Shaders` folder.

2. Double-click on the new shader to open it in your code editor.

3. Select all the autogenerated code and delete it. Then, add the following code:

```
Shader "ARCoreDesign/UnlitShadowReceiver"
{
 Properties
 {
  _Color("Main Color", Color) = (1,1,1,1)
  _MainTex("Base (RGB)", 2D) = "white" {}
  _Cutoff("Cutout", Range(0,1)) = 0.5
 }
 SubShader
 {
  Pass
  {
   Alphatest Greater[_Cutoff] SetTexture[_MainTex]
  }
  Pass
  {
   Blend DstColor Zero Tags{ "LightMode" = "ForwardBase" }
   CGPROGRAM
   #pragma vertex vert
   #pragma fragment frag
   #include "UnityCG.cginc"
   #pragma multi_compile_fwdbase
   #include "AutoLight.cginc"
   struct v2f
   {
    float4 pos : SV_POSITION; LIGHTING_COORDS(0,1)
   };
   v2f vert(appdata_base v)
   {
```

```
    v2f o;
    o.pos = UnityObjectToClipPos(v.vertex);
    TRANSFER_VERTEX_TO_FRAGMENT(o);
    return o;
    }
    fixed4 frag(v2f i) : COLOR
    {
      float attenuation = LIGHT_ATTENUATION(i);
      return attenuation;
    }
  ENDCG
  }
}
Fallback "Transparent/Cutout/VertexLit"
}
```

4. This shader is an example of a transparent shadow receiver. The shader works in two passes. In the first pass, we essentially clear the texture based on a cutoff alpha value. This allows us to turn an object transparent and still receive a shadow. The second pass draws the shadow using a vertex and fragment shader. Feel free to spend time studying this shader further.

 As ARCore matures, there will likely be more versions of transparent shadow receivers available. Plan to search for other options or other ways to improve this form of shader in the future.

5. Save the file and return to Unity.
6. Create a new material in the `Assets/ARCoreDesign/Materials` folder and name it as `UnlitShadowReceiver`. Set the properties of the material, as shown in the following excerpt:

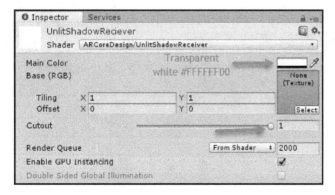

Setting the properties on the UnlitShadowReceiver material

7. Select and drag the `armchair` prefab from the `Assets/ARCoreDesign/Materials` folder in the **Project** window and drop it in an open area of the **Hierarchy** window. We want to adjust our prefab a bit, and this is the easiest way.

8. From the menu, select **GameObject | 3D | Plane**. Expand the `armchair` object and drag the **Plane** onto the **24 Ligne Roset Citta armchair** child object.

9. Select **Plane** and reset the position to (0, 0, 0) and scale to (0.1, 1, 0.1) on the **Transform**. Set the material to new **UnlitShadowReceiver**, as shown in the following excerpt:

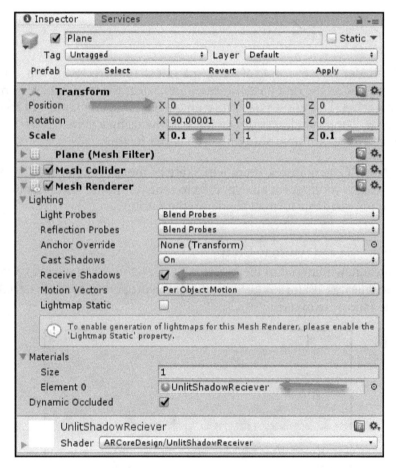

Setting the Plane material to UnlitShadowReceiver

10. Select the armchair object in the **Hierarchy** window and then in the `Inspector` window, click on the **Apply** button beside the **Prefab** properties to save the prefab. Leave the prefab in the scene for now, but we will want to delete it later.

We just created our transparent shadow receiver shader and then set it on a plane that we added to our prefab. We need to do this in order for our object, the `armchair`, to correctly cast a shadow on our new transparent receiver. Next, we need to turn on shadows, as the ARCore example has them disabled by default.

Turning the shadows on

Follow along to turn shadows back on:

1. Select the **Directional Light** in the **Hierarchy** window and set the lights properties as shown:

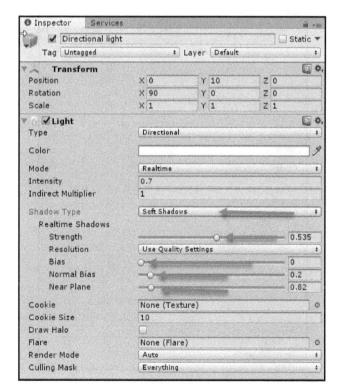

Turning on shadows for the Directional Light

2. As soon as you change the **Shadow Type**, you should see an immediate change in the **Scene** window with the armchair now showing a shadow underneath. If you are unable to see a shadow yet, don't panic, we likely need to just adjust the quality settings.

The ARCore example uses a blob texture for a shadow on the Andy model. By updating this to use a shader, we now have automatic support for any object you want to add. Just remember to adjust the plane to the object. If you wanted to add a painting or other wall hanging, you would set the plane vertical with the object.

3. From the menu, select **Edit | Project Settings | Quality**. Set the **Android** build to use the highest quality settings by **Default** by clicking on the arrow icon underneath the **Levels** for **Android**. This is shown in the following excerpt:

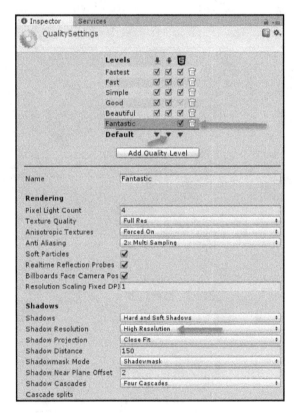

Setting the Quality setting for the build

4. Make sure and apply the changes to the prefab again. This just assures us that are changes are saved before we delete the prefab from the scene.

5. Select and delete the `armchair` object from the scene.

> We are using the highest quality settings in this example. For the most part, ARCore apps will run on relatively new devices, which means we can attempt to push the limits. If you find that the quality settings are crashing your device or not rendering correctly, then try dropping the quality on the build a level. You may want to do this anyway to improve your app's performance.

6. Connect, build, and run. Place a chair and see the difference, as shown:

Example of the complete app with lighting and shadows

This is as far as we will go with the app in this chapter. Feel free to enhance the app on your own and take time to complete some of the optional exercises on your own. If the shadow doesn't show up correctly go back and edit the shadow settings on the light and the quality settings.

Exercises

Answer the following questions on your own:

1. Change the model in the app to the `sofa` or even another object.
2. Add the changes we made to the `Environmental Light` script in order to track the light direction.
3. Add other objects to the app and allow the user a choice on which to place.
4. Allow the user to place vertical objects. Hint—you will need to render vertical planes now, yes ARCore does recognize vertical planes.
5. Allow the user to rotate the model. Hint—you may have to add some control handles.

Summary

With that, we have completed our simple example of a design app. We were able to complete all the major technical items we wanted to accomplish. We started with setting up a new Unity project using the ARCore example as a template. This saved us some time in what would have otherwise become a very long chapter. Next, we learned how to import new models from sites such as `TurboSquid` and how to set them up as prefabs for later use. Then, we built a simple UI to allow us to clear the tracking planes from the view and clear any models. After that, we added the ability for a user to select and move an object in the AR scene. This required us to enhance one of the ARCore example shaders and heavily modify the `SceneController` script. Finally, we tackled shadows by turning on lights and adding a transparent shadow receiver to our object prefab.

ARCore is well suited for the next wave of HoloLens or mixed reality low-cost headsets. In the next chapter, we take a bit of a break from AR and dive into mixed reality, where we will build a multiplayer app called `HoloCore`.

10
Mixing in Mixed Reality

Mixed reality (MR) is the evolution of combining **augmented reality** and **virtual reality** into the same experience or app. MR typically uses a wearable device to overlay the virtual world on top of the user's reality. The concept first gained traction with Microsoft's introduction of HoloLens. HoloLens is a wearable glasses device that allows you to overlay your real world with virtual content using hand gestures, not unlike what we have been doing with ARCore in this whole book, except the difference of the wearable part and, of course, the price tag.

 Microsoft is currently leading the charge in mixed reality development with their platform of the same name, which is great exposure for the whole AR/VR and now MR space. Microsoft is a big technology company and, like many big technology giants, has decided to redefine the concept of mixed reality to also include virtual reality.

Wearable devices that allow users to experience mixed reality have been traditionally quite expensive, until just recently. Through group funding and other initiatives, there are now plenty of cheap, less-than $30 US wearable devices out there that will allow you to experience MR. This is perfect for anybody who wants to dive in and learn how to develop MR apps. Of course, not all MR platforms are designed for mobile devices, or will work with ARCore. Fortunately, an open source project called **HoloKit** has released a cardboard MR headset that is designed to work with ARCore.

"I'm not confused. I'm just well mixed."
                                        - Robert Frost

In this chapter, we will build a combined AR / MR ARCore app that will be meant as a technology and learning demo that showcases the power of AR and MR. We will, of course, need to get our feet wet a little with VR as well, which should make things interesting. The following is the list of main items we will focus on in this chapter:

- Mixed reality and HoloKit
- Introducing WRLD
- Setting up WRLD for MR
- Navigating the map
- Mapping, GIS, and GPS
- What's next

This is a really big chapter with lots of material to go over. Unfortunately, we cannot include the content in a completed package due to licensing. However, we have tried to write each section in this chapter so that it can be used on its own, almost like a cookbook. This will allow you to pick and choose the components you want and don't want to use.

 To best experience the exercises in this chapter, it is recommended that you obtain a HoloKit. You should be able to obtain this device for around $30. If you are feeling adventurous, there are even plans available to build your own. Here's a link to where you can learn more about HoloKit and order your own at `https://holokit.io/`.

Mixed reality and HoloKit

HoloKit was created by Botau Hu, a brilliant new tech innovator that will surely experience great success in the industry. It's a *wearable* device that projects your mobile devices screen into a 3D holographic projection. This holographic projection is then overlaid onto the user's view, thus allowing them to experience a more immersive environment that often teeters on the edge of VR. The following is an illustration of what a HoloKit looks like fully assembled:

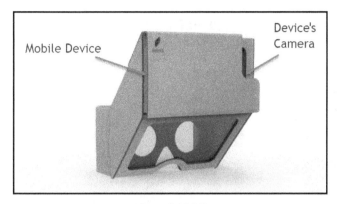

Fully assembled HoloKit

As you can see from the diagram, the device is quite similar in construction to that of Google Cardboard. Cardboard was Google's way of democratizing VR to the masses, and it worked. If you are unable to quickly get a HoloKit, you can also use a modified Google Cardboard. Just cut a slot in the cardboard for the device's camera and ensure not to move around too much.

One of the first things you will note about most mixed reality headsets is the ability of the user to see through their environment. This allows the user to still be spatially aware of their surroundings, while experiencing what could be an almost virtual experience. Since a user is more aware, MR devices are generally considered safer, and the user is much less prone to experiencing motion sickness and/or falling down. Currently, VR devices are not considered appropriate for those under the age of thirteen due to those issues.

VR motion sickness is often more a result of poor app performance or resolution. As it turns out, visual artifacts caused by a lagging app or poor resolution are responsible for placing additional strain on the user's brain. That strain will then manifest itself in the form of a severe headache or nausea. In the early days of VR, this was a big problem, but now the technology has improved enough for most users to be able to use an app for several hours at a time.

The **Mirage Solo** headset was developed by *Lenovo* for a game by Disney called *Jedi Challenges*. Jedi Challenges is really more a proof of concept and showcase for mixed reality and what is possible. It will likely also be a collector's item, since it is associated with the new Star Wars franchise and just happens to correspond to an up-and-coming tech revolution. The only truly unfortunate thing about this project is that Lenovo never released a developer kit; hopefully they will rectify this is in the future.

The following is an image of the Lenovo Mirage Solo headset:

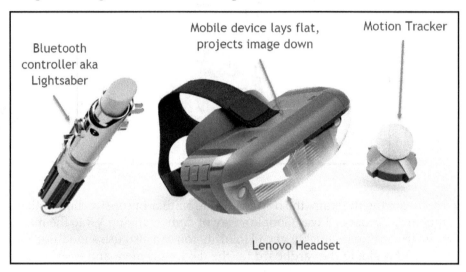

Jedi Challenges Mixed Reality game

In order to complete the exercises in this chapter, you won't need HoloKit. HoloKit allows for you to switch from AR to MR/VR mode at the press of a button. This means that you can still work through all the exercises in this chapter. However, it does mean that you won't experience the magical experience of MR. In the next section, we set up HoloKit to work with ARCore and get ready to build our tech demo.

Setting up HoloKit

The great thing about HoloKit is that it comes complete with its own Unity template project. This makes our job of getting up and running with HoloKit quite painless. Open up Command Prompt or a shell window and do the following:

1. If you haven't already done so, create a new folder from the root called `ARCore` and navigate to it:

   ```
   mkdir ARCore
   cd ARCore
   ```

2. Clone the HoloKit repository into it:

   ```
   git clone -b android https://github.com/holokit/holokitsdk.git
   ```

3. That command clones the specific **Android** branch, which we will use. HoloKit is also supported for **ARKit** on **iOS**.

4. Open a new instance of the Unity editor. Create and open a new project called `HoloCore` in the `ARCore` folder.

5. In the **Project** window, create a new folder under **Assets** called `HoloCore`. Under that new folder, create our standard five new folders (`Scripts`, `Scenes`, `Materials`, `Models`, and `Prefabs`).

6. Open the `ARCore/holokitsdk/Assets` folder with a file explorer window. Make a copy of the `HoloKitSDK` folder and place it in the `ARCore/HoloCore/Assets` folder. When you are done, return to the editor, and you should see the assets getting imported and compiled. After the import is complete, confirm that your **Project** window resembles the following:

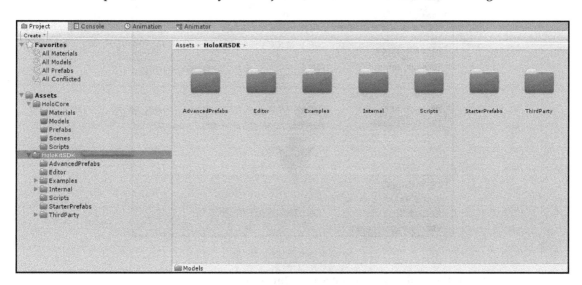

Project window folders showing HoloKitSDK

7. If you are prompted to switch to **Android**, elect to do so by clicking on **OK**.

8. From the menu, select **Edit** | **Project Settings** | **Player**. This will open the **Player** (as in app player) settings panel. Select the **Android** tab and uncheck the **Multithreaded Rendering** option, and set the **Package** name, **API Levels**, and **ARCore Supported**, as shown:

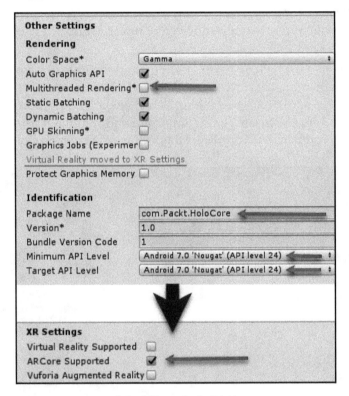

Setting the Player settings for Android

9. Open up the **HoloKit** sample scene CubeOnTheFloor in the Assets/HoloKitSDK/Examples folder.

10. From the menu, select **File** | **Save Scene as**, and save the scene as **Main** in the Assets/HoloCore/Scenes folder.

11. Open up **Build Settings** and add the current scene to the build.

12. Connect, build, and run. You should see a rather small button in the top corner with the letter **C**. Press that button to switch from **AR** to the **MR** mode. When you are ready, put your device into the HoloKit headset and enjoy your first MR app.

Unlike Google Cardboard, HoloKit needs to let the camera view the user's surroundings in order to track. As such, you may need to modify the headset by cutting out a larger hole for the device's camera to see through. Here's a pic of a HoloKit that needed to be modified in order to accommodate a Samsung Galaxy S8:

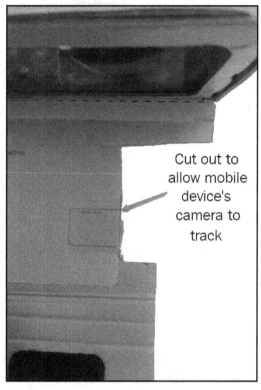

Cut out to allow mobile device's camera to track

Modified HoloKit to allow camera to visibly track

If you have another device that you want to hack, like Cardboard, then just ensure that you cut a space so that the camera is not blocked. Some other mixed reality headsets that work with mobile devices already have camera extensions. These camera extensions may support a fish eye lens, which allows for the device to see a wider area. This works quite well, since it essentially converts the camera into a sensor with a wide angle lens.

How does it work?

Before we get too far ahead of ourselves, let's break open the HoloKit project and take a look at how or what it does. Open up the Unity editor and complete the following:

1. Find the **HoloKitCameraRig** in the **Hierarchy** window, and then select and expand it. Expand the children's children and so on until you can see the **Left Eye** and **Right Eye** objects, as shown in the following screenshot:

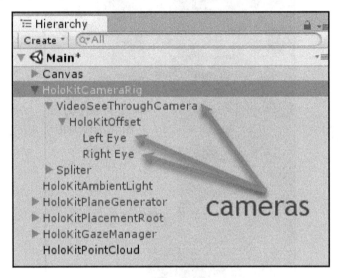

View of the scene's 3 cameras in the Hierarchy window

2. The **VideoSeeThroughCamera** is the main camera used when the app is in AR mode. When the app is in **MR** mode, the **Left Eye** and **Right Eye** cameras are used to create the stereo 3D vision. Take a closer look at the **Eye** cameras, and you will note that their position is slightly adjusted on the x axis. For the right camera, the amount is **0.032**, and for the left it is **-0.032**. This is how we generate 3D stereo projections, using an offset camera for each eye.

3. The other components are as follows:
   - **HoloKitAmbientLight**: It is just a standard directional light with the ARCore Environmental Light script attached.
   - **HoloKitPlaneGenerator**: It is a base object for the HelloARController script, which we have seen plenty of before.
   - **HoloKitPlacementRoot**: It is our main anchor point for the scene's virtual objects.

- **HoloKitCameraRig**: It is what controls the app view.
- **HoloKitGazeManager**: It is new and allows the user to select objects just by positioning their gaze or view on the target. You can try this now with the current scene and the ball. Fix your gaze on the ball and see what happens.
- **HoloKitPointCloud**: It serves the same function as its counterpart in ARCore.

4. Go through and continue to expand and inspect the rest of the objects in the scene.

5. Connect, build, and run the scene again. This time, pay attention to the details and see if you can get the **Gaze** to work.

Well, hopefully that was relatively painless. Now, with HoloKit setup, we have the framework in place for our combined AR and MR app. We should expand on what our tech demo will do. The premise of our tech demo will be an app that allows the user to move between a traditional map interface and an AR or MR interface. The name HoloCore is a play on the ability to allow a user to drill into a map and render a 3D view in AR or MR. This also nicely ties in with the name ARCore. In the next section, we will look at adding a 3D map of the world to our app.

Introducing WRLD

Mixed reality apps, because they provide spatial awareness to the user, are excellent for viewing massive objects or areas like a map. Unlike virtual reality, mixed provides a more intuitive and natural interface for movement since the user can also physically move their position. So, what better way to fully explore MR than by using it to view a 3D map of the world. Fortunately, there is a relative newcomer called **WRLD** that has started to make significant waves in AR / VR and MR, because it provides an excellent and simple solution for rendering a fairly-good 3D map.

 WRLD is a great platform for general 3D mapping and visualization. It currently does not support more robust backend GIS services, but it certainly could. For those professional GIS developers with access to Esri CityEngine, there are also some great workflows for bringing CE models into Unity. This means that you can also experiment with CE models in MR.

WRLD is shipped as a Unity asset right to the **Asset Store**, so installation is a breeze. However, before we install, we need to go to the WRLD site and get a developer account. WRLD is a commercial service that charges by usage. Fortunately, they offer free developer access for a limited, which is perfect for our tech demo. Open up a browser and complete the following:

1. Browse to `wrld3d.com` and **Sign Up** for an account. Ensure that you verify the account through email.
2. Return to the site and **Sign In**.
3. Find and click on the **Developers** link at the top of the page. This will take you to the **Developers** page.
4. Click on the big **Access API Keys** button at the top of the page.
5. Enter the name for your key, `HoloCore`, and click on **Create API Key** to create the key, as shown in the following screenshot:

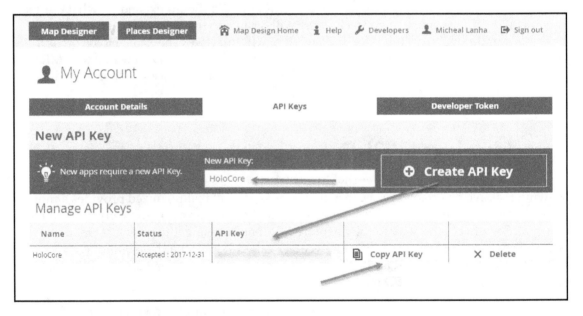

Creating a WRLD API key

6. Click on **Copy API Key** to copy the key to your clipboard. We will use it shortly.
7. Return to the Unity editor and, from the menu, select **Window | Asset Store**. This will open a browser page inside the editor.

8. Enter WRLD in the search box and click on the **Search** button. This will open the asset page for WRLD, offering you to **Download** the asset. Click on the **Download** button, as shown in the following screenshot:

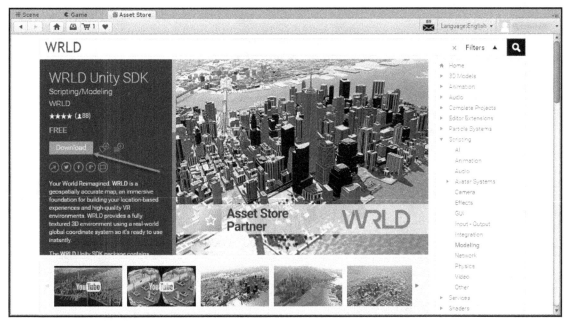

Downloading the WRLD asset from the Asset Store

9. This will download the package. After the package downloads, you will be prompted with an asset import dialog. Just click on **Import** to import everything. This may take a while, so stretch your legs and grab some refreshments.

 In some cases, you may want to be more careful on what you bring into your projects. For instance, if you were building a non-tech demo or proof of concept, you would likely remove any sample scenes or other excess from a project. We will talk more about keeping projects lean in Chapter 11, *Performance Tips and Troubleshooting*.

10. You may get a warning prompting you that the versions don't match with your version of Unity. Accept the warning and continue.

11. When you are prompted to get a key after you import WRLD, just click on **Later**. After all, we already have a key.

12. Next, you will probably be prompted to increase the shadow distance with the following dialog:

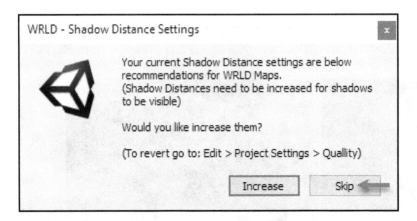

Skip the Shadow settings dialog

13. Click on the **Skip** button. We will need to adjust the lighting, materials, and shadows later manually.

This imports the WRLD asset into our project. In the next section, we will cover how to set it up and run WRLD for our MR app.

Setting up WRLD for MR

With the asset imported, we can now work on setting up WRLD to work in MR. The setup requires a little bit of customization, so jump back to Unity and complete the following:

1. From the menu, select **Assets | Setup WRLD Resources For | Android**. This will ensure that the assets are optimized for **Android**. We will also talk, in a later section, about how the materials can be manually optimized by updating or creating your own shaders.

2. Ensure that the **Main** scene is loaded, and then select and expand the **HoloKitPlacementRoot**. Disable the **DebugCube** and **GazeTargetExample** child objects. If you forgot how to do this, check the **Inspector** window.

3. Create a new child GameObject of **HoloKitPlacementRoot** called WRLD. Go to the **Inspector** window and use **Add Component** to add the Wrld Map component to the object.

4. Set the component properties of the `Wrld Map`, as shown:

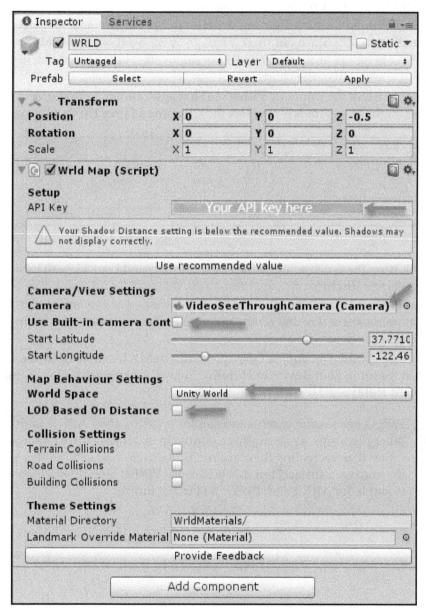

Setting properties for the Wrld Map component

5. Select and drag the new WRLD object into your Assets/HoloCore/Prefabs folder to create a prefab that we can use later.

6. Select **HoloKitCameraRig** from the **Hierarchy** window and set the **Transforms Y Position** to 300. Since our map is at 0, 0, 0, we want our viewer to look down from a height of around 300 meters or about 1000 feet. Then, expand the object until you see all of the children.

7. Select each of the cameras, **VideoSeeThroughCamera**, **Left Eye**, and **Right Eye**, and, in the Inspector window, set the **Clipping Planes Far** to 5000, as illustrated:

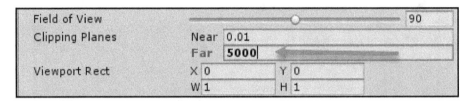

Setting the Far plane clipping distance

8. Adjusting the far clipping plane essentially expands our view to include all objects to a distance of 5000. Previously, this was set for 1000. You may also want to increase the **Near Clipping Plane** to a larger value; 1 to 10 works well. If you note a slight flashing on the map, this is likely caused by the clipping plane being set to close.

9. Connect, build, and run. Set the app to run in **MR** by clicking on the **C** button and then inserting your device in HoloKit. Enjoy the experience of viewing a map in mixed reality.

 WRLD has several excellent examples on using their API on Unity and other platforms. We built this example in order to feature mixing realities, rather than recreating their examples. As such, we have omitted placing the map on a surface, but this is because WRLD already has a good example for ARKit and, likely, will in the future.

What you just experienced is quite fun, especially considering the minimal effort this example took to get setup, except that there are several things missing. Most certainly, we want to be able to move and zoom in and out of our map, so we will cover movement and navigating in the next section.

Navigating the map

In a traditional AR app, you rarely move the user or player. The user or player move themselves, and the AR app works around that. We spent a good portion of this book understanding how ARCore tracks the user and understands their environment, which has worked quite well when working with small objects such as Andy. Except, if we want to render massive virtual objects or even embed new environments, then we need a way for the user to navigate those as well. Therefore, in this section, we will look to implement a mix of navigation methods from a standard touch interface to AR and MR versions. If you don't have a HoloKit or are not interested in trying MR, then you can stick to just working with the AR.

Before adding navigation to our app, we probably should look at how navigation is handled by default in WRLD. Open up the Unity editor and follow along:

1. Save your current scene.
2. Create a new scene. Name it `Navigation` and save the scene in the `Assets/HoloCore/Scenes` folder.
3. From the `Assets/HoloCore/Prefabs` folder, drag the `WRLD` prefab we created earlier and drop it in the scene. Set the properties on the `Wrld Map`, as shown in this screenshot:

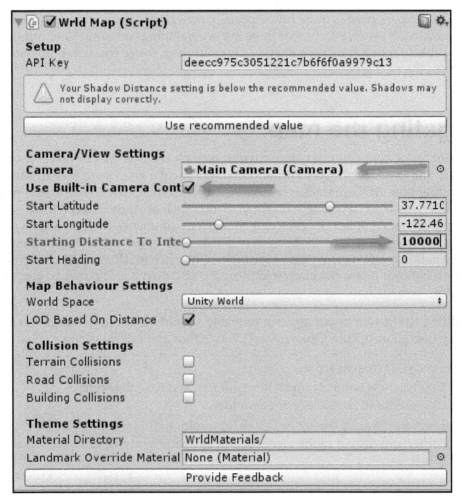

Setting properties for the WRLD prefab

4. This is more or less the default settings that you will use to just render the map to your device in a non-AR interface.

5. Open the **Build Settings** dialog and add your new scene to the build. Uncheck the **Main** scene, but don't delete it; we will turn it back on later.

6. Connect, build, and run. You will now see the map as the main element in your view. You can use touch gestures to move, pan, and zoom the map.

As you can see by playing with the app, the map navigation is very slick using the touch interface. We will use this to allow the user to navigate the map with touch until they see an area of interest that they want to take a close look at. Then, they will be able to switch to **AR** or **MR** mode to view the items in more detail. In order to do this, we will use the scene we just created as our starting scene, and use our **Main** scene to let the user switch to **AR** or **MR**.

 Being able to switch between interface types like a regular touch-driven UI and AR or MR works all the time. An excellent example of this, of course, is the popular game *Pokemon Go* from Niantic Labs. This also happens to use a map and allows a user to switch to AR to catch Pokemon. If you are curious about how Pokemon Go was constructed, take a look at the book *Augmented Reality Game Development* by *Micheal Lanham*, also from *Packt*.

Switching from AR to MR

Being able to switch scenes and maintain state is common task, but it seems to require a bit of work in Unity. Open up the Unity editor to the `Navigation` scene and complete the following:

1. Open up the `Assets/HoloCore/Scripts` folder and create a new script called `Singleton`. Go to the book's downloaded source `Code/Chapter_10` folder, copy the contents of the `Singleton.cs` file, and paste it into your new script. A `Singleton` is common pattern in Unity for creating an object you only want one of and when you never want that object destroyed. If you are new to `Singleton`, it will be in your best interest to spend some time and review the class.

2. Create a new script in the same folder called `SceneController` and replace the generated code with the following:

```
using System;
using UnityEngine;
using UnityEngine.SceneManagement;
using Wrld;
using Wrld.Space;
namespace Packt.HoloCore
{
  public class SceneController : Singleton<SceneController>
  {
    protected SceneController() { }
  }
}
```

3. SceneController is a Singleton with a SceneController. That circular reference may be a little confusing, so it is best to think of as a SceneController that is a Singleton which holds the SceneController type. Inside the class, we need to define a protected default constructor in order to force access through the Instance. We will look at how to use Instance shortly.

4. Enter the following right after the constructor:

```
public LatLongAltitude position;
```

5. Next, we will add a single property to hold the position where the camera was last fixed. That way, when we switch scenes, we can just pass the position property back to the scene so that it can determine where to setup. LatLongAltitude is a spatial data type that holds the position of the camera in latitude, longitude, and altitude.

6. Add the following new method, LoadScene, with the following code:

```
public void LoadScene(string scene, Camera mapCamera)
{
    if (Api.Instance.CameraApi.HasControlledCamera)
    {
        mapCamera = Api.Instance.CameraApi.GetControlledCamera();
    }
    if(mapCamera == null) throw new ArgumentNullException("Camera",
"Camera must be set, if map is not controlled.");

    position = Api.Instance.CameraApi.ScreenToGeographicPoint(new
Vector3(mapCamera.pixelHeight/2, mapCamera.pixelWidth/2,
mapCamera.nearClipPlane), mapCamera);

    SceneManager.LoadScene(scene, LoadSceneMode.Single);
}
```

7. `LoadScene`, is where all the work happens. We will call `LoadScene` on the `SceneController`, passing in the `scene` name we want to load at the current `map` or WRLD camera. Inside the method, we first test to see whether the current `map` is being controlled; if it is, we just ignore the camera and use the controlled camera. Next, we test whether the `mapCamera` is null; if it is, we want to exit with an error. Otherwise, we extract the current position with `ScreenToGeographicPoint`. This method extracts the camera's main screen focal point, which we assume is at half pixel width and height of the screen; `mapCamera.nearClipPlane` sets the front of view frustum or camera if you recall from our earlier discussions, which equals the altitude of the camera above ground level, or the map in this case. At the end of the method, we use `SceneManager`, which is the Unity helper class for loading scenes. We call `LoadScene` with the option to replace the scene using `LoadSceneMode.Single`.

That completes our `SceneController`. Now, the useful thing about being a `Singleton` is that we never have to physically add the component, because it is now always considered available. WRLD bases most of their Unity API on this pattern as well. We do still have to add some further code that can be activated from our scene.

Building the SceneSwitcher

Let's add another script/component that will just activate our `SceneController`. Open up the editor and complete the following:

1. Create a new C# script called `SceneSwitcher`, and replace all the pre-generated code with the following:

```
using UnityEngine;
namespace Packt.HoloCore
{
    public class SceneSwitcher : MonoBehaviour {
    }
}
```

2. Create the following property inside the class:

```
public Camera mapCamera;
```

3. This is a placeholder for the `mapCamera`, the camera being used to render the `Wrld map`. We need this when the map is not being controlled by the camera, which is the case when the user is in AR / MR.

4. Then, create the following method:

```
public void SwitchScenes(string sceneName)
{
    SceneController.Instance.LoadScene(sceneName, mapCamera);
}
```

5. This method will be responsible for using the `LoadScene` on the `SceneController`. Note the use of `Instance` in between the class and method call. Remember that our `SceneController` is a `Singleton`, which is an object and not a static class. Therefore, we need an instance, and that is provided with a helper property called `Instance` in `Singleton` and so when calling a method on `SceneController`, we always call it through `Instance`.

6. Save all your files, if you haven't already done so, and return to Unity. Ensure that you have no compiler errors.

Creating the SceneSwitcher prefab

With the code complete, it is now time to build our `SceneSwitcher` prefab. Open the editor to the `Navigation` scene and complete the following:

1. From the menu, select **GameObject | UI | Canvas**. Add the `SceneSwitcher` component (script) to the canvas and rename it as `SceneSwitcher`. Set the **Map Camera** property on the `Scene Switcher` to use the **Main Camera**.

2. Select the **SceneSwitcher** object in the **Hierarchy** window and then, from the menu, select **GameObject | UI | Panel**. Set the properties of the panel, as shown in the following excerpt:

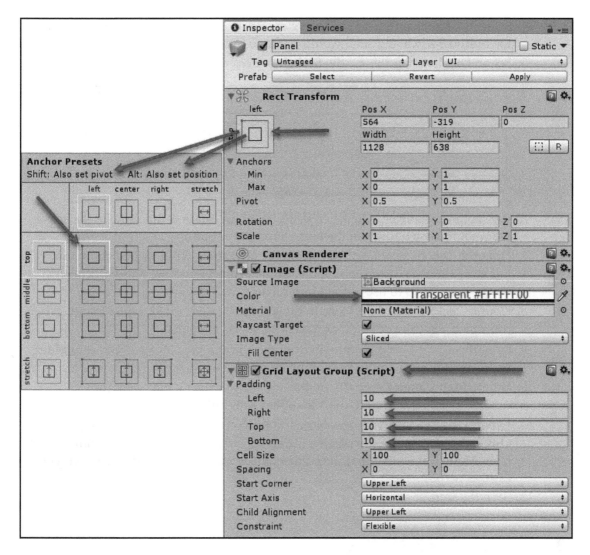

Setting the properties on the Panel

3. Set the **Anchor** by clicking on the button and then, when the **Anchor Presets** menu opens, simultaneously press the pivot and position keys (*Shift* + *Alt* on Windows) and then click on the top-left corner. This will set the panel to anchor to the top left. You will also need to add a **Grid Layout Group** component and set the properties specified.

4. Select the **Panel** and, from the menu, choose **GameObject** | **UI** | **Button**. Rename the button **Switch** and set the button text to **Switch**.

5. Set an **OnClick** handler for the **Switch** button, as follows:

Adding a button OnClick handler

6. We set the parameter, which is a string, to **Main**. **Main** is the name of the scene we want to switch to when the user clicks on the button.

7. Drag the SceneSwitcher object from the **Hierarchy** window and drop it into the Assets/HoloCore/Prefabs folder of the **Project** window. This will create a new prefab for us to use in the **Main** scene.

8. Double-click on the **Main** scene in the Assets/HoloCore/Scenes folder. When prompted, save the Navigation scene changes, of course.

9. Drag the SceneSwitcher prefab from the Assets/HoloCore/Prefabs folder and drop it into an empty area of the **Hierarchy** window.

10. Set the **Map Camera** property on the SceneSwitcher component (on SceneSwitcher object) to the **VideoSeeThroughCamera**.

11. Expand the SceneSwitcher object and locate the **Switch** button. Change the **OnClick** event handler to pass Navigation, which is the scene we want to load from **Main**. Remember that the scene names must match exactly, so watch your case.

12. Save the scenes.

Modifying the Wrld map script

We are almost done; the last thing we need to do is let the `Wrld Map` script pull the last camera's position from our singleton `SceneController`. This means that we unfortunately have to modify the source of the `Wrld Map` script. Generally, we want to avoid modifying a third-party API, except that we have the source, and it really is our only option. Open up the `WrldMap` script, located in the `Assets/Wrld/API` folder, and follow along:

1. Insert the following, between the lines identified:

   ```
   using Wrld.Scripts.Utilities;   //after me
   using Packt.HoloCore;
   #if UNITY_EDITOR   //before me
   ```

2. Scroll down to the `SetupApi` method and insert the following code between the lines identified:

   ```
   config.Collisions.BuildingCollision = m_buildingCollisions; //after
   me
   config.DistanceToInterest =
   SceneController.Instance.position.GetAltitude();
   config.LatitudeDegrees =
   SceneController.Instance.position.GetLatitude();
   config.LongitudeDegrees =
   SceneController.Instance.position.GetLongitude();
   Transform rootTransform = null; //before me
   ```

3. All this does is set the map to the last position the camera was pointed at. You can see that we are using the `SceneController` singleton here to access the camera's last known position. You can see in the `SetupApi` method where a configuration object is defined and set. Hopefully, in the future, `Wrld` allows for this configuration to be passed into the script. If that was possible, we could just modify that configuration before it is passed to the `WrldMap` script, thus eliminating the need for us to add our own code in the class.

4. Save the file and return to Unity. Check for any errors.

5. Open the **Build Settings** dialog and ensure that both scenes are added, active, and in the order shown in the following excerpt:

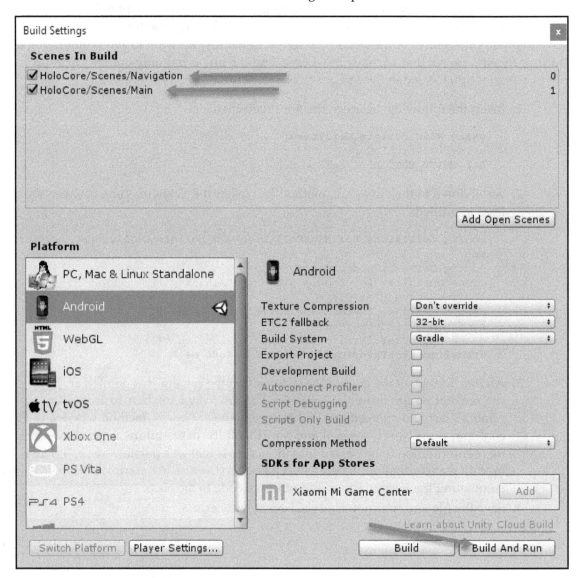

Setting the scenes and scene order on Build Settings dialog

6. Connect, build, and run the app. Since we are starting at 0, 0 in latitude and longitude spatial coordinates, the map will start just off the coast of Africa, which is 0, 0. Use a pinch touch gesture to zoom out until you see the global view of the world. Use a touch slide gesture to pan the map to North America, currently the best place to view WRLD data. Choose an area that is familiar and zoom in until you start to see 3D objects. Then, press the **Switch** button to switch the interface to **MR** and **AR**. You can switch back to the **Main** view by pressing **Switch** again. The following is an image showing the augmented reality mode and another user using the mixed reality mode with a **HoloKit** headset:

Augmented reality view of the application running

7. We now have an app that lets a user navigate a map and then switch to view areas of interest in **AR** or **MR** mode. This works well, except that it would be better if the user started at their current position. In order to do that, we need to understand a bit more about mapping, GIS, and GPS, which we will cover in the next section.

Mapping, GIS, and GPS

Unity, as we already learned, tracks its objects in 3D space using a point with a **Cartesian** coordinate reference system of x, y, and z. When we plot a point on a map of the world, it is no different; we need to reference the point, except that now we need to use a spherical or **geographic** reference system to represent a position on the earth, because as we all know, the earth is spherical. However, converting between a geographic system and Cartesian system is expensive. Many mapping applications, therefore, use an intermediary reference known as **earth-centered, earth-fixed** (**ECEF**), which represents mapping data on an earth-fixed Cartesian coordinate reference system. The following is a diagram shows the differences between Cartesian, geographic, and ECEF coordinate reference systems:

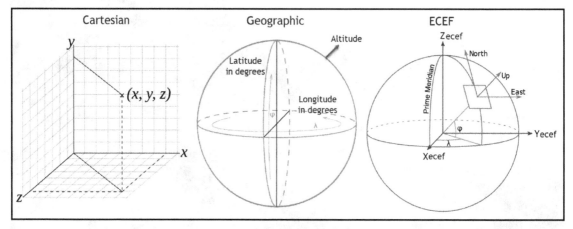

Comparison of coordinate reference systems

Now, you may have already noticed that WRLD supports ECEF out of the box. As we mentioned, since ECEF is already in a Cartesian frame of reference, the conversions are much easier and quicker. However, for us, we just want to position the camera at the user's geographic coordinate reference, which we can easily obtain from the user's device using GPS.

Accessing the user's GPS on their device takes a bit of work, but fortunately, we can do this all in one place. Let's open up the `SceneController` script and make the following modifications:

1. Add two new properties at the top of the class:

```
public bool isLoaded;
public string status;
```

2. Create a new method just under the constructor:

```
void Awake()
{
   StartCoroutine(GetLocationPoint());
}
```

3. The `Awake` method is a special Unity method that runs when the `GameObject` first initializes. Inside of the method, we are calling `StartCoroutine`. `StartCoroutine` is another special method in Unity that allows you to create a `coroutine`. `Coroutines` are a way of interrupting or breaking your code flow, doing something else, and then returning to complete your original task. In the call, we are passing in a method call `GetLocationPoint()`, which sets up that method as a `coroutine`.

4. Add the following method to create the `coroutine`:

```
IEnumerator GetLocationPoint()
{

}
```

5. A coroutine must return `IEnumerator`. By adding the return type, the method can now `yield` or interrupt its execution with a `yield return` statement that returns a `YieldInstruction`. We will see how to do that shortly.

6. Just inside `GetLocationPoint`, add the following line:

```
AndroidPermissionsManager.RequestPermission(new string[] {
"android.permission.ACCESS_FINE_LOCATION" });
```

7. This line of code prompts the user for access to the `location` services, also known as GPS. We do this in order to explicitly identify the user's `location`, provided that their device's GPS is not being blocked or the user has the `location` service disabled.

 Google has developed their own `location` service in essence by mapping wireless endpoint MAC addresses to geographic coordinates. Google does this by essentially war driving with its self-driving Street View cars. While those cars drive themselves around, they are also grabbing the MAC address of every wireless device that they can detect at the time of mapping that to a GPS `location`. As it turns out, this service can actually be more accurate for providing `location` in more dense metropolitan areas where GPS line of sight is difficult.

8. Then, add the following:

```
if (Input.location.isEnabledByUser == false)
{
    isLoaded = true;
    yield return SetStatus("Location not authorized, starting at
0,0", 1.0f);
    yield break;
}
```

9. This block of code checks whether the user had GPS enabled; if they don't, there is nothing we can do. We set `isLoaded` to `true`, which will be a flag to let outside methods know that we found or didn't find a `location`. Then, we `yield return` the results of a call to `SetStatus`. Remember that because we are in a `coroutine`, `yield return` means that we want to interrupt code execution at this point.

10. Scroll down just past the `GetLocationPoint` method and add the following new method:

```
public YieldInstruction SetStatus(string status, float time)
{
    this.status = status;
    return new WaitForSeconds(time);
}
```

11. Inside the method, we are setting our `status` text, which will be a message we want to display back to the user. Then, we return a new `WaitForSeconds(time)`, where `time` represents the number of seconds to wait. There are many different forms of `YieldInstruction` that you can use to break your code. The `YieldInstruction` here just waits for a set number of seconds and then returns to continue the code where it left off. Keep in mind that after the `yield` has elapsed, for whatever reason, code will then resume from exactly where it left off.

12. Return to where we left off in `GetLocationPoint`. Right after the `yield return SetStatus` call, we are executing `yield break`. This line breaks the `coroutine` and exits the method, which is equivalent to return in a normal method.

13. Now that we understand `coroutines`, let's enter the next section of code:

```
yield return SetStatus("-----STARTING LOCATION SERVICE-----", 1);
Input.location.Start();

// Wait until service initializes
```

```
int maxWait = 30;
while (Input.location.status == LocationServiceStatus.Initializing
&& maxWait > 0)
{
  yield return new WaitForSeconds(1);
  maxWait--;
}
```

14. First, we start by setting a `status` message and letting the user know that we are starting the service, which we then do. After that, we continually loop, breaking every second with `yield return new WaitForSeconds(1)`, adjusting our counter `maxWait` for every iteration. We need to wait for the `location` service to initialize; sometimes this can take a while.

15. Enter the following code to handle when our counter has expired (`maxWait<1`):

```
// Service didn't initialize in 20 seconds
 if (maxWait < 1)
 {
   yield return SetStatus("ERROR - Location service timed out,
setting to 0,0,0", 10.0f);
   isLoaded = true;
   yield break;
 }
```

16. Inside the `if` block, we set the `status` and `loaded` flag. Then, we return from the `coroutine` with `yield break`.

17. Next, we want to handle when the service fails or starts by entering the following:

```
if (Input.location.status == LocationServiceStatus.Failed)
{
  yield return SetStatus("ERROR - Unable to determine device
location.", 10.0f);
  isLoaded = true;
  yield break;
}
else
{
  //set the position
  yield return SetStatus("-----SETTING LOCATION----", 10.0f);
  position = new LatLongAltitude(Input.location.lastData.latitude,
Input.location.lastData.longitude,
Input.location.lastData.altitude);
  isLoaded = true;
}
```

18. This code handles the service failure or success. In the failure path, we set an error message and exit. Otherwise, we set a `status` and wait for `10` seconds. We do this so that the user can read the message. Then, we set the position according to the geographic coordinates the device provides us with.

19. Finally, we stop the service with this:

```
Input.location.Stop();
```

21. We stop the service because we don't need to continually get `location` updates. If you want to keep the service open and use it to track the user's `location`, such as Pokemon Go, then just ensure that you stop the service when the object is being destroyed. You can do this in a method called `OnDisable()`, which is another special Unity method that is used to clean up the object.

22. At this point, we also want to update and overload the `LoadScene` method with the following code:

```
public void LoadScene(string scene)
{
    SceneManager.LoadScene(scene, LoadSceneMode.Single);
}

public void LoadScene(string scene, Camera mapCamera)
{
    if (Api.Instance.CameraApi.HasControlledCamera)
    {
        mapCamera = Api.Instance.CameraApi.GetControlledCamera();
    }
    else if (mapCamera == null) throw new
ArgumentNullException("Camera", "Camera must be set, if map is not
controlled.");
    position = Api.Instance.CameraApi.ScreenToGeographicPoint(new
Vector3(mapCamera.pixelHeight / 2, mapCamera.pixelWidth / 2,
mapCamera.nearClipPlane), mapCamera);

    Debug.LogFormat("cam position set {0}:{1}:{2}",
position.GetLatitude(), position.GetLongitude(),
position.GetAltitude());
    SceneManager.LoadScene(scene, LoadSceneMode.Single);
}
```

23. We overloaded the method in order to allow two different behaviors when switching scenes. The new method we added won't worry about setting the `position` for the camera. We also added some logging, so we can see what values are being set by looking at our Android debug tools while running the app.
24. Save the file when you are done.

The code we just set up was originally derived from the Unity sample, but it has been modified for your reuse. Since accessing the `location` service can take a while, we will add a new scene in order to handle the `location` service starting up. This will be a splash screen that you can make prettier later on.

Making the Splash scene

The `Splash` scene we are building is very basic for now, with just some status messages. You can, of course, style it and add any images you like later on. Open up the editor and complete the following:

1. Create a new scene called `Splash` and save the scene to the `Assets/HoloCore/Scenes` folder.
2. From the menu, select **GameObject | UI | Panel**. This will add a new **Canvas** with a child **Panel** and **EventSystem**. Set the background color of **Panel** to a dark gray.
3. Select the **Panel** and, from the menu, select **GameObject | UI | Text**. Change the name of the object to `Status` and set its properties in the **Inspector** window, as shown:

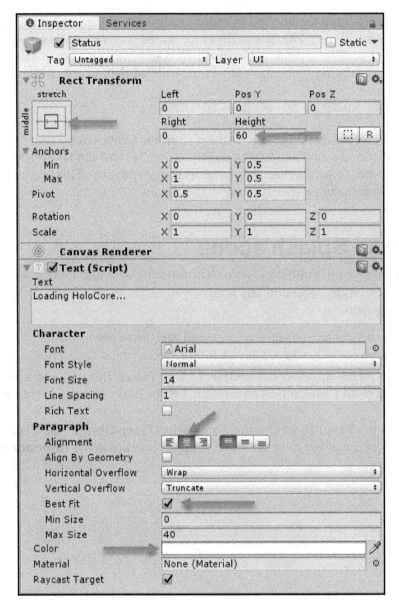

Setting the Status text properties

4. This is the where we will display those status messages back to the user, which means that we need a script that can update the status messages as well as know when the service has been loaded and the application can start.

5. Create a new C# script called `SceneLoader` in the `Assets/HoloCore/Scripts` folder and replace the pre-generated code with the following:

```
using UnityEngine;
using UnityEngine.UI;

namespace Packt.HoloCore
{
  public class SceneLoader : MonoBehaviour
  {
    public string sceneName;
    public Text statusText;
    void Update()
    {
      if (SceneController.Instance.isLoaded)
      {
        SceneController.Instance.LoadScene(sceneName);
      }
      else
      {
        statusText.text = SceneController.Instance.status;
      }
    }
  }
}
```

6. This simple class is what we will use to track the status of our `SceneController`. All the action takes place in the `Update` method. We first check whether the `SceneController` has loaded by testing `isLoaded`. If the scene has not loaded, we display the `status` text in the `statusText.text` object. Remember that the `Update` method is run every rendering frame, so we are testing this condition several times a second. Save the script, and next, we need to add it as a component to our scene.

7. Return to the Unity editor and wait for the new class to compile.

8. Create a new object called `ScreenLoader` and add the new `ScreenLoader` script to it. Then, set the properties of `SceneLoader` to what is shown here:

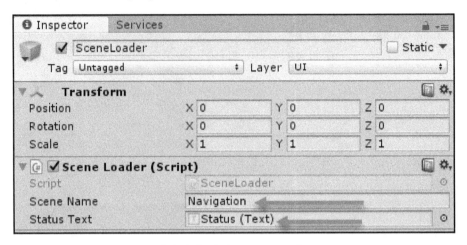

Setting the SceneLoader component properties

9. Set the **Status Text** property to the `Status` object. You can use the bull's-eye icon to select the object from the scene or just drag the object from the **Hierarchy** window and drop it into the slot.

10. Save the scene.

11. Open **Build Settings**, add the `Splash` scene to the build, and ensure that it is the first scene, as follows:

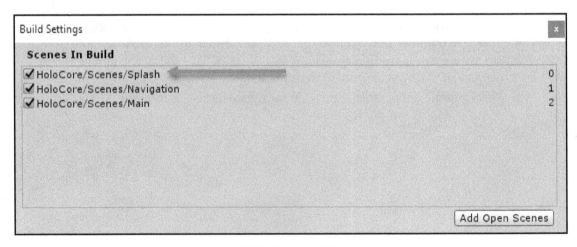

Adding the Splash scene to the build

12. Go ahead, connect, build, and run. You will now be taken to `location` as identified by the `Location` service, that is, if you allow the service to connect.

Fixing the altitude issue

You may notice an issue if you live above 500 meters above sea level. This issue happens because our AR camera is fixed at 500 meters altitude. The problem is that we have our AR camera at a fixed height; we now need to adjust that based on the camera's altitude. Open back up the editor and complete the following:

1. Create a new C# script and replace the code with the following:

```csharp
using System.Collections;
using System.Collections.Generic;
using UnityEngine;

namespace Packt.HoloCore
{
    public class SceneCameraMover : MonoBehaviour
    {
        void Awake()
        {
            var altitude =
SceneController.Instance.position.GetAltitude();
            transform.position = new Vector3(0f, (float)altitude, 0f);
        }
    }
}
```

2. This script creates a new class called `SceneCameraMover`. The job of `SceneCameraMover` is to move the AR camera into position when the view switches to AR / MR.
3. Save the script and return to Unity.
4. Open the **Main** scene from the `Assets/HoloCore/Scenes` folder.
5. Expand **HoloKitCameraRig** and select **VideoSeeThroughCamera**. Then, add the script to the component using **Add Component** and searching for **SceneCameraMover**.
6. Set the **Transform** on the **HoloKitCameraRig** to 0, 0, 0. We will now let the script move the camera to the position we need.

7. Save the scenes and project.

8. Connect, build, and run. Go to an area that is well above sea level, say the mountains, and switch to AR / MR view. The camera should now position itself correctly based on the altitude you were viewing the scene at.

Ensure that you explore other areas of interest around the world. In the next section, we will finish up the chapter and our discussion of AR and ARCore with the next steps, and we'll see where you can go to build your own incredible tech demo or commercial app.

 The online example demos from WRLD recommend using an alternate streaming camera for AR visuals in ARCore or ARKit apps. However, we found that adding an alternate camera, alongside the already two additional cameras for the HoloKit, caused the app to be more unstable than it already can be. If you don't plan to use MR or HoloKit, you likely want to experiment with the alternate streaming camera.

What's next?

The tech demo we developed is an excellent example of the possibilities of integrating technologies across user experiences. This has already been done extensively, and one popular example is Pokemon Go. In fact, you can say that Pokemon Go put AR into our vocabulary. So what is the next big AR app you will develop with ARCore? Are you still trying to think of some ideas or possibilities? The following is a list of app ideas or industries that are investing heavily in AR right now:

- **Entertainment (Games)**: Gaming and entertainment is the most competitive space you can be in. Developing an app for this space requires hard work and a bit of luck. There have been some grand successes in this space, but that was after some hard work and considerable backing.

- **Healthcare (Emergency services)**: The healthcare industry is diving into the AR / MR and VR world in full force. Since this industry is heavily funded, it is now a leader in these technologies. If you want to get into cutting-edge reality development, this is the space to be in. It can be more difficult to get into, since this industry has traditionally been more isolated, but now there are plenty of opportunities with the explosion of growth.

- **Marketing (Retail)**: As AR becomes more mainstream and readily available, we will come across new apps developed in this space. There have already been some great novel concepts used to encourage sales, which have worked, except that AR has become something of a novelty in this space as of late. However, if you talk to anyone in marketing, they will agree that some day a majority of advertising will be provided via AR. Until then though, perhaps you can think of the next great app that will sell hamburgers.

- **Education (Knowledge transfer)**: This is another really big industry that can be hard to get into, that is, if you are planning to put your app in a classroom. Alternatively, you can build an educational app that perhaps teaches you how to cook but is delivered through an app store. Either way, this can be a difficult industry to get into but very rewarding, especially if you like teaching or learning.

- **Military**: It's very difficult to get into, unless you have a military background or other established credentials. This likely means a strong educational background as well. This is an interesting industry if you can get in, and is certainly not for everyone. If this is your choice though, you will most certainly be working on cutting-edge apps or tools.

- **Travel & tourism (History)**: This one crosses over with education, as some of the same principles may apply. Perhaps, it is showing someone a historical battle over the area where the real battle took place. There are plenty of opportunities for developers of all skill levels to work in this area building AR / MR apps.

- **Design (All)**: This one can tie in a lot with retail applications. Perhaps demonstrating an outfit overlaid onto someone's body or trying to determine whether a chair works in a room. We put this further down in the list because our expert survey listed this one lower as well. However, as we demonstrated, ARCore has plenty of great design applications.

- **Industrial (Manufacturing)**: Applications of AR can help human users as well as provide better foundations for future automation of systems or other processes. This means that the AR systems we build for humans now will also help us make the manufacturing robots of the future smarter.

- **Automotive**: We have already seen AR system in automobiles for a few years now. From heads-up displays to GPS devices, this industry has already embraced AR, although it isn't likely that developing an embedded AR app for this industry makes a lot of sense. Most users, drivers, would likely prefer to use an AR off their device. Perhaps it makes more sense for the automotive industry to provide a docking station for a mobile device in vehicles with an AR interface?
- **Music**: Think of this as more for the musician and not the audience. This is a set of AR tools that help musicians compose and work with music. Not for everyone and not well suited to ARCore, perhaps they will embed voice recognition or other audio recognition into ARCore someday.

Whatever you plan to build as your next app, we sincerely wish you the best of luck and would eagerly like to hear about any great apps. Be sure to contact the author with your great app concepts.

Exercises

Complete the following exercises on your own:

1. Go back to the `HoloCore` example and track the user's position with a block or sphere. Hint—the first part of this example is in the code download.
2. Track the user's position as they move on the map. Hint—you will now need to update the user's position from the most recent GPS readings.
3. Track multiple users' positions around you. Hint—you can use the Firebase Realtime Database to track the user's position in geographic coordinates.

Summary

For this chapter, we diverted away from AR a little and explored mixing augmented and mixed reality. We discovered that we can easily experience mixed reality apps with a simple device called a HoloKit or other cheap headset. ARCore tracks the user well and is a great fit for adding the MR experience. Who knows, in the future when everyone is wearing MR glasses, will we even distinguish AR and MR as different? We then set up the HoloKit template app and went to work building a quick MR demo. After that, we expanded on our demo by adding in WRLD. WRLD, as we learned, is a fun and easy-to-use API that can quickly give us some large-scale impressive 3D scenery that is representative of the user's area. From there, we developed a number of scenes for all the users to move a map touch interface to a full mixed-reality view of the map, where we were able to obtain the user's geographic coordinates from their device's GPS and put them at the same position in WRLD. Finally, we looked to the future and industries that you can focus your app development skills on.

We complete our journey in the next chapter with a discussion of performance and troubleshooting, both of which will be helpful as you grow your skills to become a better AR developer.

11
Performance Tips and Troubleshooting

This will be the end of our journey of exploring **ARCore** and augmented reality. In this chapter, we will look at general performance tips for AR and mobile apps specifically. Then, we will cover a number of troubleshooting solutions to use when and/or if you encounter any problems. We will speak about the possible specific issues you may encounter as well as more general patterns to follow if you encounter problems. Here's a summary of the main topics we will cover in this chapter:

- Diagnosing performance
    - Chrome DevTools
    - Android Profiler
    - Unity editor
- Tips for better performance
- General troubleshooting
- Troubleshooting tips

As you likely have already noted many times throughout this book, AR apps require a high level of performance in order to provide a compelling user experience. In the next section, we will look at how we can diagnose performance with each of our platforms.

Diagnosing performance

In this section, we will look at the specific steps you will need to take in order to diagnose performance for each of our development platforms (web, Android, and Unity). It is often easy to lose track of performance, especially when working with new or unfamiliar technologies. Therefore, you often want to include some form of performance assessment as part of your development process, perhaps even implementing some minimum frame rate warnings for when your app is rendering at subpar performance or frame rates. Before we get into designing a performance test though, we want to understand how to track performance in each platform, starting with the web using **Chrome DevTools** in the next section.

Chrome DevTools

One of the pleasures you will have when developing web projects with ARCore is the ease of debugging with Chrome. In fact, if you were doing a comparison, web project performance tooling would be ranked #2 on our platform list due to the capabilities of Chrome DevTools. Let's open up the `spawn-at-surface.html` web example from `Chapter 5`, *Real-World Motion Tracking*, and perform the following steps:

1. Start `http-server` on port `9999` in the `Android` folder, just like we did previously.
2. Pick an **endpoint** that matches your local network and write or copy it for later. Remember that your device and development machine need to be on the same network for this to work.
3. Launch the **WebARCore** app on your device and navigate to your selected endpoint. This will often look something like `http://192.168.*.*:9999`, where the `*.*` will be replaced by your development machine's specific IP.
4. With **WebARCore**, navigate to `http://[YOUR IP]:9999/three.ar.js/examples/spawn-at-surface.html`.
5. Connect your device to your dev machine, either remotely or with a USB cable.
6. Return to your machine and launch Chrome. Open the **Developers tools** with *Ctrl* + *Shift* + *I* (*command* + *option* + *I* on Mac).
7. Click on the **Remote Devices** tab and select your device. Then, click on the **Inspect** button to open another Chrome window with `WebView` of the app running on your device.

8. Click on the **Performance** tab and then select the **Record** button to start **Profiling**, as shown in the following screenshot:

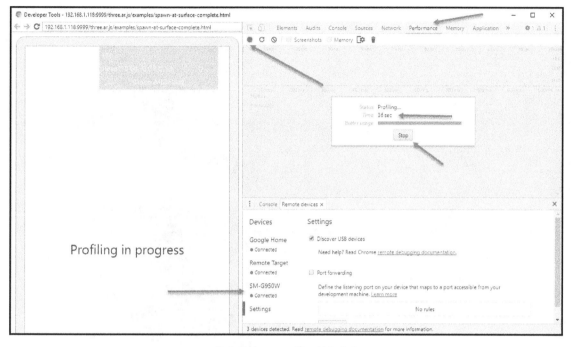

Starting performance profiling with DevTools

9. Let the app run in your device with the **Profiler** running for around 30 seconds and then click on **Stop**. After you stop capturing the data, a profile session will expand in the **Timeline** window.

If you find that the **Profiling** session keeps crashing, disable the **Screenshots** feature by unchecking the box at the top of the window.

10. Click on the **Call Tree** tab at the top of the **Summary** window, as follows:

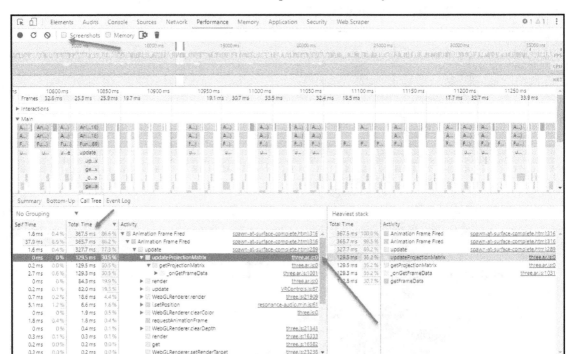

Profile session timeline

11. The **Call Tree** tab is where you can quickly identify function calls or sections of code that may be causing performance issues. In our example, we have drilled into the update function and can see that the bulk of the time spent inside this function is building the projection matrix with a call to updateProjectionMatrix. Since this call resides within the three.ar.js library, it is not something we will concern ourselves with.

12. Feel free to continue testing and profiling. Try setting several **Andy** models and see what impact this has on performance.

With any performance profiling, the thing you will want to quickly identify is spikes or areas where you see data peak. Identifying why these spikes take place will help you understand what activities can impact performance. Placing an **Andy**, for instance, will cause a spike due to the instantiation of a model into the scene. You will also want to closely watch how the app recovers from a spike. Does the app, for instance, fully recover, or only recover partially?

If you are transferring data or doing **AJAX** calls in your web app, then you will also want to monitor **Network** performance. The **Network** tab has a tool interface similar to that of the **Performance** tab.

After identifying spikes, you will want to expand your view to cover the whole session. Then, you can expand the **Call Tree** and identify the most time-consuming methods. Chances are that if your app is spending 80% of its time in a single function, then you need to be very careful about what operations take place in that function. Finding and optimizing expensive methods can often get you very quick gains in app performance. While the tools are different, the same principles apply for all our development platforms.

We have just started to scratch the surface for what is possible with the DevTools. If you are doing any amount of web development, you will quickly get up to speed with these tools. In the next section, we will cover the Android profiling tools.

Android Profiler

Android Studio has great performance profiling tools; after all, it provides the closest metal-to-metal interface with your mobile Android device. However, it is not as simple to use as the DevTools and therefore comes a close third in comparison to other profiling tools. We will use one of the sample Android projects we worked with. Open up **Android Studio** and either of the `java_arcore_hello_ar` or `android` (TensorFlow example) sample projects, and perform the following steps:

1. Connect your device and build the app to your device. Wait for the app to start running on the device.

2. From the menu, select **View** I **Tool Windows** I **Android Profiler**. This will open a profiling tool window, as shown in the following screenshot:

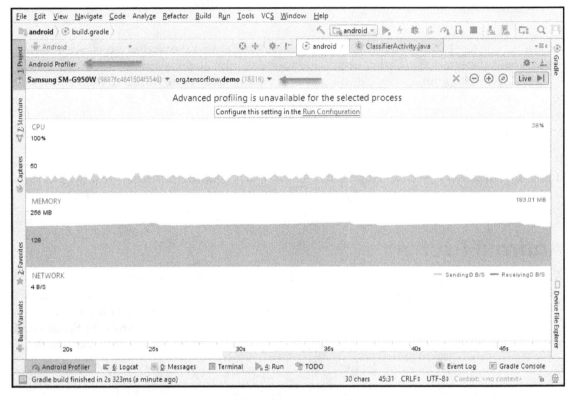

Android Profiler capturing a real-time session

3. As the app runs, watch the **MEMORY** and **CPU** usage. You can click on any point in the plots in order to expand the view and look at the call stack and various other views of the code execution, as illustrated in the following screenshot:

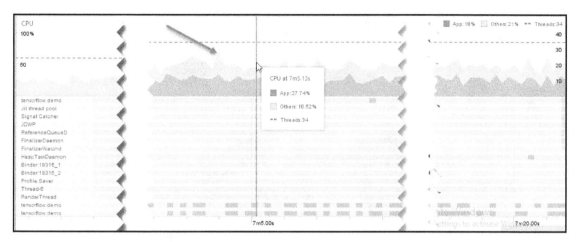

Inspecting the real-time profiling session

4. You can also record sessions for later inspection by pressing the **Record** button at the top of the **Profiler** window.

At this point, you can look for performance spikes or the general overall performance of various function calls using **Android Profiler**, just like you did with Chrome. The Android tools are more difficult to learn and use, but they're well worth the effort if you are doing any serious Android/Java development. In the next section, we look at our final way to profile performance, with Unity.

Unity Profiler

Unity is a powerful tool with a very powerful profiler tool that is a pleasure to work with and explore, not just for profiling, but it also provides an insight into the inner workings of Unity. Open up the Unity editor to one of the sample projects we have worked with. For this example, we will use `HoloCore` from `Chapter 10`, *Mixing in Mixed Reality*, but feel free to use another app if you prefer. With the editor open, perform the following steps:

1. From the menu, select **Window** | **Profiler**. The window will open undocked. Drag the window over by the tab and drop it beside the **Game** window tab to dock it on the right. Normally, we would dock the **Profiler** beside the **Inspector** so that you can watch the profiling while running a game in the editor. Since we can't run ARCore apps in the editor, for now, we will give the **Profiler** more room by docking it next to the **Game** window

2. Open the **Build Settings** dialog and check whether the **Development Build** and **Autoconnect Profiler** settings are enabled, as shown in the following screenshot:

Setting Development Build settings

3. Connect your device with a USB, build, and run. Leave the app running on your device.

4. Return to the editor and open the **Active Player** dropdown and select **AndroidPlayer(ADB@127.0.0.1:someport)**, as shown here:

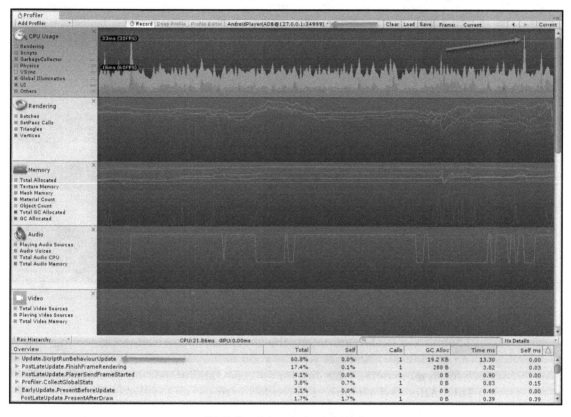

Unity Profiler capturing session from Android device

5. Click on one of the spikes, as shown in the preceding screenshot. With the **CPU** panel selected, direct your attention to the bottom **Details** panel.

6. Use the dropdown to select **Timeline**, as follows:

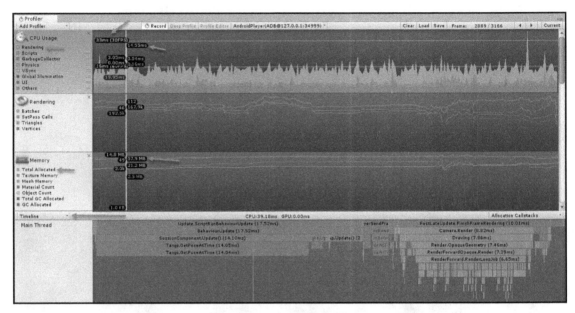

Inspecting the details of a profiling session

7. There is plethora of useful information here, and it can certainly be overwhelming at first. Fortunately, the Unity interface is self-documenting, and you can quickly get a sense of what is good or bad. We will go over what areas to watch for in more detail later, but for now, pay attention to the **Rendering** time and **Total Allocated Memory**. For rendering times, you will usually see a number in **ms** or milliseconds in time and **FPS** or frames per second. A good rule is to ensure that your frame rate stays above **30 FPS**. A memory can equally be critical when building for mobile apps.

8. When you are profiling, put the app under stress by changing between reality modes, if you are using `HoloCore`, for instance. Then, continue drilling into the various detail panels and watch how values change at various points of the app session.

The Unity tools provide the most powerful and intuitive interface for profiling your app. While we barely scraped the power of all the tools we looked at, you will note that they all bear a strong resemblance. Of course, this is not by accident and after you learn the ins and outs of performance profiling an app on one platform, a number of those skills will carry over. In the next section, we will look at a list of tips for better app performance.

Tips for managing better performance

Now that we have a grasp on how to profile our apps, let's take a look at the primary items that will impact performance. The order of these items is ordered by general importance, but the individual requirements of your app may alter these priorities. Feel free to consult the following checklist the next time you need or want to profile your app:

- **Rendering (includes all CPU and memory resources responsible for rendering a frame)**:
    - **Render loop (CPU performance)**: Check the timing of the `render` function and watch for any expensive calls. Ensure that you minimize any object instantiation, logging, or inner loops. Remember that the render function, typically called `Update`, will be called 30 times per second or more. All the tools we looked at will let you perform this vital task.
    - **Frame rate (render time)**: Outside of optimizing your code, the frame rate will often be dictated by the complexity and number of objects we are rendering. As such, you may want to go as low as optimizing shaders, but many times, you can get great performance gains by reducing the number of triangles or complexity of your models. In a mobile app, this means looking for low poly simple models as assets. Another useful option is to build various **Levels Of Detail** (**LOD**) for your model and use the appropriate version for the appropriate detail level. Unity provides an excellent set of free and paid assets for LOD optimization that can make this task easy.
    - **Lighting and materials**: Not only will the complexity of a model impact performance but also the textures or materials (shaders) and lights you are using to render the model. Ensure that you limit the size of textures or ensure that all your shaders have a fallback or simplification. You will also want to simplify lighting where possible.

- **Memory (graphics)**: As a general rule, the more memory your app is using, the more expensive a frame will be to render. Of course, there are exceptions, but watching the memory can pinpoint potential issues or even memory leaks. A high memory will often point to models, textures, or other assets that may need optimization.

- **Loading (the process of adding, replacing, or updating new content in the scene)**:

  - **Object instantiation**: Large complex meshes with multiple detailed textures will require extra load times. You will often want to cache or preload objects in order to reduce interruptions during loading. For most of our examples, this wasn't an issue, but a good example of where this was a problem was in Chapter 10, *Mixing in Mixed Reality*, where we used the 3D map.

  - **Streaming**: Streaming is a great way to load media resources such as audio or video to play just the content you need. In Unity, setting a resource to stream instead of loading completely is fairly easy and can be done at the resource definition, as shown in the following screenshot:

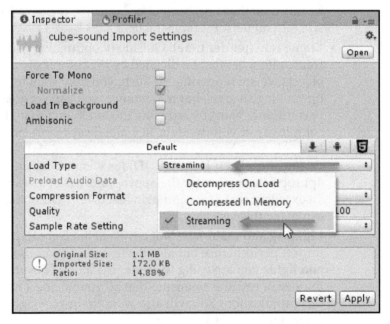

Enabling streaming on an audio resource

- **Garbage collection**: All of our platforms manage object lifetime through some form of garbage collection while the app is running. Keeping the number of objects you create and destroy to a minimum will alleviate pressure on the GC. If the GC fills up quickly, this will often trigger an expensive collection operation, which may freeze your app. You can reduce object instantiation and collection by creating object pooling. Object pooling is where you keep a stock of objects in memory, adding and removing objects from the scene as you need.

- **Interaction (includes any activity by the user or the environment, be it physical or artificial)**:
    - **Environment detection**: This is a requirement more specific to AR apps and crucial to ARCore. If you are planning to augment detection of point clouds or planes, ensure that you optimize this code as much as possible.
    - **Object interaction (physics)**: Limit the number of objects that you need to test for ray casting or collisions. You can do this by tagging your objects and then filter the tags. In Unity, this feature is built in, but it is fairly easy to implement for other platforms.
    - **AI (machine learning)**: If your app needs to do any AI for an **non-player character** (**NPC**) or other agent, then you may want to limit any expensive calls for AI or learning. Instead of running your AI for every frame, you may want to limit it to every fifth or tenth frame, for instance. Often, this has the added benefit of making the AI more realistic or smarter, since it appears to think for a short period before action.

The preceding list is a good place to start when looking for possible performance problems, and it should suit you well as a guide for any platform you need to profile. In the next section, we will cover some general troubleshooting tips that you can use for each platform when developing.

General troubleshooting

We learned the basics of the debugging process for each platform, but we never covered any techniques for debugging or troubleshooting. Just like profiling, there is a basic guide or list that you can follow to make you more efficient when troubleshooting. Use the following list of steps to help you troubleshoot your next issue:

1. **Console**: The first place to look is for any errors that are being reported to the console. All our platforms provide a console, and you should be familiar with accessing it on your platform of choice. Does the error make sense? Are you able to pinpoint the section of code or item causing the issue?

2. **Google**: If you see an obscure console message and are not quite sure what it does, then Google it. You don't want to Google the entire message, but just extract five or six key words in the phrase and use those. You may also want to add words to cover your platform; for instance, Java, Android, or, Unity C#.

3. **Logging**: Instrument your code by injecting logging statements in key areas of your code. If your code is not reporting errors to the console, put in logging to let you know where the code flows. This can help you determine if and when key sections of code are being run.

4. **Replicate**: Isolate the problem and try to replicate it in a new project or test app. If you are unable to isolate the code, you have a bigger issue, and you should probably refactor. Generally, unless the issue requires a workaround or is something more serious, replicating the project can solidify your understanding of the issues. Replicating an issue cannot only help you solve the problem, but it can also help you refactor and clean your code.

5. **Post it**: If you still don't have a resolution after replicating the problem then look for the appropriate forum and post your issue. Ensure that you provide your replicated sample when you post your issue. It will often be the first thing someone will likely ask you for, especially if the problem is complex. Also, showing that you spent time replicating the problem will make your post more credible and avoid the wasted time of responding to simple questions.

6. **Work around it**: If you can't resolve your issue, then work around it. Sometimes, resolving your issue is not possible or just too expensive and time consuming. Then, you will need to come up with another way to either build the feature or alter it. This will often require going back to the designer or visionary, if your project has one, and consulting them for some possible workarounds.

The preceding list is again a good place to start when you encounter an issue. If you have been developing software for some time, you will likely have your own process, but the preceding list is probably not much different from yours.

Troubleshooting code

For those of you with less experience in troubleshooting code, follow this simple exercise:

1. Open the Unity editor to a new blank project and starting scene.
2. Create a **Cube** object in the scene.
3. Select the **Cube** and in the **Inspector** window, click on **Add Component**. Select **New Script** and the set the name to Test and then click on **Create and Add** to add the script to the object, as follows:

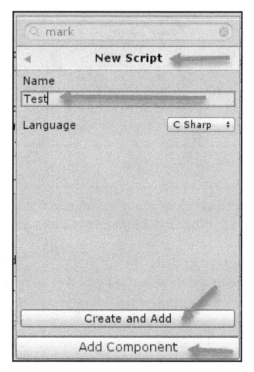

Creating a new script with Add Component

4. This will create a script in the root Assets folder. It's not the best place to drop a script, but this method is useful for creating quick test scripts.

Try to avoid writing replication/test or proof of concept code in your main development project. Keep your main project as clean as possible. If you are building anything commercial, you will most certainly want to go through the extra effort of validating every asset or resource in your project or at least the ones you are responsible for. It is a useful team exercise to go through your references and assets on a regular basis, perhaps once a month or more frequently if you are making multiple changes.

5. Open the `Test` script in an editor of your choice and add the following highlighted lines of code:

```
using UnityEngine;
public class Test : MonoBehaviour {
    public GameObject monster;   //add me
    // Use this for initialization
    void Start () {

    }

    // Update is called once per frame
    void Update () {
        if(monster.transform.position.x > 5)   //and add this section
        {
            Destroy(this);
        }
    }
}
```

6. This script simply tracks a `GameObject` called `monster` and determines when its x position exceeds 5. When it does, the script destroys its parent object with `Destroy(this)`.

7. Save the file and return to Unity.

8. Add another **Cube** to the scene and rename it to `Monster`.

9. Press the **Play** button at the top of the editor to start the scene.

10. Click on the **Console** window to bring it to the top. Watch the stream of errors, as illustrated in the following screenshot:

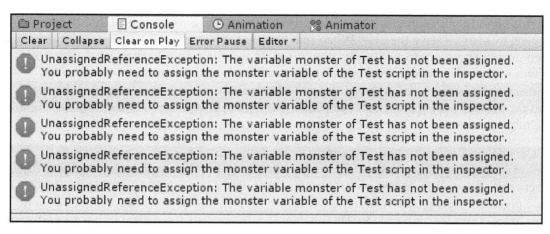

Console window showing a stream of errors

11. So, the general error message we are seeing is **UnassignedReferenceException**. Quickly Google that text to see what comes back in the results. Did that give you any more insights other than the message on the **Console**?

Chances are that you may have already solved the issue, but let's continue as if we are still stumped. Say, for instance, the Google result was far less helpful. Follow along to continue our troubleshooting (debugging) process:

1. Our next step is logging. Add the following line of code just inside the `Update` method:

```
Debug.LogFormat("Monster is at position ({0})",
monster.transform.position);
```

2. This line of code outputs a debug message to the **Console**.
3. Of course, running the code again will replicate the same issue, which also means that you just replicated the problem, and cover the next step in a single line of code.

While logging is good, it can also be bad, for performance and anyone trying to hack your game. You can usually control the level of logging you want to output for each environment. As a general rule though, try to avoid excessive logging unless the information is required or useful.

At this point in our example, it should be self-explanatory as to what the issue is, but of course, this isn't always the case. When that happens, if you have exhausted all other paths, then post the problem to an appropriate forum. If nothing comes back in time, then you may need to move on and work around the problem. Strangely enough, it is often not unusual to be halfway through writing a workaround to realize your mistake. It happens, and the best advice is to just move on. Failure is a great way to learn and the more you fail, the more you learn.

In Canada, you are taught how to winter drive in the ice and snow by going out to a parking lot and spinning around and losing control. While this can certainly be lot of fun, it teaches the driver how to lose control under controlled poor weather conditions. This not only gives the driver more confidence, it also reinforces how to control a vehicle when it loses traction under high speeds. Then, when the driver does lose control, they can attempt to avoid or minimize damage. Unit testing your code is not like learning how to winter drive. It tests the limits of your code so that you can be sure what will happen if something works or fails.

Most developers struggle with the concept of adding unit test code to their game or graphics projects. In fact, the practice is discouraged by the lack of tools or knowledge available. Unit testing or rigorously testing your code is never a waste of time, and using a testing framework for your platform will go a long way to make this an easier task. Now whether you decide to write unit tests for your code or not is up to you, but you should learn how to unit test. The practice of just learning how to test your code will open your eyes to a world of possibilities.

The more you code and develop games or other applications, the better you will get at troubleshooting errors. There is no substitute for practical experience. In the next section, we will look at more specific troubleshooting items that you may have encountered during the course of the book.

Exercises

Complete the following exercises on your own:

1. Alter the `if` statement that checks the monster's position so that the code avoids the error entirely.
2. Are you able to fix the unassigned reference issue in code? Hint—check out the `GameObject.Find` method.
3. Write a monster script that moves its block using the keyboard or mouse as input.

Troubleshooting tips

There is a lot that can go wrong when working with any new technology, not only because of your lack of familiarity, but it may also happen that the technology may not be prepared to do all the things it claims it can do. Here's a table of common issues you may encounter while working through the book:

Platform	Issue	Resolution
Web	Unable to load page or find server	Check whether you are using the correct endpoint for your machine. If you have a few choices, try a different option. Confirm that your system does not have a firewall running that could be blocking the communication. Try disabling your firewall (temporarily) and try again. If this resolves the issue, then make an exception in your firewall for port 9999 or whatever port you used.
Web	ARCore displays an error message on the page	Ensure that the ARCore service is installed and you are using the WebARCore enabled browser for your platform.
Web	Missing references	Ensure that you check that the path you are using to load content or scripts is correct. You can do this easily in Chrome by checking the **Sources** tab.
Android	Unable to build or missing references	Android Studio is very helpful, but it sometimes needs to load a lot of references. In this case, you just need to be patient and load everything the project requires. If you are building your project from scratch, you will need to refer to a good tutorial on Android project setup to do it right. If you find that you are still missing references, then create a new project and try again.
Android/Unity	Unable to connect to device	This rarely happens anymore, but it can happen on occasion. Unplug and plug your device back in or run `adb devices` at a console or shell window. If you are connecting remotely, you may have to reconfigure the device by reconnecting the USB and resetting the connection.

Unity	All compiler errors have to be fixed before you enter the play mode	Check the console for any red error messages. Double-click on any messages to be taken to the syntax error in the code. Do your best to resolve or remove the syntax error.
Unity	Unable to build	Check for any compiler errors and ensure that your scenes are added to the build with the **Build Settings** dialog.
Unity	Build stalls	If you are connected to a device and the cable disconnects momentarily, this can cause the build to lock or just stop. Usually, just clicking on **Cancel** will exit the build process, and you can just start again. On occasion, very rarely, you may need to restart Unity.

The preceding table should help you resolve more of the common show stopper issues you may encounter while traversing the book. If you encounter something outside this list, certainly consult Google or your other favorite search engine. You will often find that just rebuilding the project will teach you where you went wrong.

Summary

This is the last chapter of our book, and we spent our time well, learning about performance and troubleshooting. We first covered the use of the various performance profiling tools you may use for each of our platforms. Then, we covered a set of very basic tips for increasing your app's performance, which covered everything from frame rate to asset size. This led us to cover tips for troubleshooting basic problems and, more specifically, coding issues. We finished off with a table of helpful troubleshooting tips that you can use to consult if you encounter more specific troublesome problems.

Now that you have completed this book, you have just started your journey into discovering AR and MR. There are plenty of more good books from Packt on AR, web development, Android development, and, of course, Unity. Readers are also encouraged to seek out your local meetups on AR/VR or if there is none, create their own. Seeing what others are doing for AR or even VR development can encourage new ideas and best practices. We all, really are, just beginning an exciting journey into a new computing interface that will radically change our lives in the years to come. With the ongoing development of wearable mainstream commercial glasses coming around the corner, you should also be poised for many more changes to come in AR.

Other Books You May Enjoy

If you enjoyed this book, you may be interested in these other books by Packt:

Augmented Reality for Developers
Jonathan Linowes, Krystian Babilinski

ISBN: 978-1-78728-643-6

- Build Augmented Reality applications through a step-by-step, tutorial-style project approach
- Use the Unity 3D game engine with the Vuforia AR platform, open source ARToolKit, Microsoft's Mixed Reality Toolkit, Apple ARKit, and Google ARCore, via the C# programming language
- Implement practical demo applications of AR including education, games, business marketing, and industrial training
- Employ a variety of AR recognition modes, including target images, markers, objects, and spatial mapping
- Target a variety of AR devices including phones, tablets, and wearable smartglasses, for Android, iOS, and Windows HoloLens
- Develop expertise with Unity 3D graphics, UIs, physics, and event systems
- Explore and utilize AR best practices and software design patterns

Augmented Reality Game Development
Micheal Lanham

ISBN: 978-1-78712-288-8

- Build a location-based augmented reality game called Foodie Go
- Animate a player's avatar on a map
- Use the mobile device's camera as a game background
- Implement database persistence with SQLLite4Unity3D to carry inventory items across game sessions
- Create basic UI elements for the game, inventory, menu, and settings
- Perform location and content searches against the Google Places API
- Enhance the game's mood by adding visual shader effects
- Extend the game by adding multiplayer networking and other enhancements

Leave a review - let other readers know what you think

Please share your thoughts on this book with others by leaving a review on the site that you bought it from. If you purchased the book from Amazon, please leave us an honest review on this book's Amazon page. This is vital so that other potential readers can see and use your unbiased opinion to make purchasing decisions, we can understand what our customers think about our products, and our authors can see your feedback on the title that they have worked with Packt to create. It will only take a few minutes of your time, but is valuable to other potential customers, our authors, and Packt. Thank you!

Index

www.ingramcontent.com/pod-product-compliance
Lightning Source LLC
Chambersburg PA
CBHW080633060326
40690CB00021B/4910